TOMORROW'S PARISH

Donal Harrington

Tomorrow's Parish

a vision and a path

COLUMBA PRESS

First published in 2015 by
coluмβλ press
23 Merrion Square North,
Dublin 2, Ireland

This revised edition, 2018

Cover design by Alba Esteban I Columba Press
Origination by Columba Press
Printed by Jellyfish Solutions

ISBN 978 1 78218 341 9

TABLE OF CONTENTS

FOREWORD

BY ARCHBISHOP DIARMUID MARTIN

The presence of the Church in Irish society has changed to an extent we could not have imagined a few decades ago. Change is threatening, but for people of faith, a time of change is a time of opportunity. It is an opportunity to examine how effectively we carry out the mission of the Church in today's world and how we look towards the world of tomorrow. We live in a society that seems less interested in religion, or even in God – a society that wonders whether God matters at all. This means that people of faith can be talking a different language to that of society at large, almost like a foreign language.

Christianity, however, is a religion of the Incarnation. Just as the infinite God took flesh in Jesus, so the Church of Christ takes flesh in each age, in a way that speaks to that age, and dwells in that age, and is at home in that age but which also rises above and enlightens the culture of any age.

The message of Jesus Christ is always one of newness. We have to rediscover that newness in every age. We have to purify our Church from factors that impede that newness from breaking through. The first disciples at Pentecost were inspired to speak in ways that people could understand in their own language. We, today's disciples, seek the inspiration to speak eloquently, with our lips and with our lives, so that the language of our faith can echo with the language of people in today's world.

The way forward is not by looking backwards, by taking refuge and becoming entrenched in the past. The Church cannot retreat into being a safe comfort zone for the likeminded. The way forward is not by some tweaking here and there. The God of newness is calling us to be courageous, to be creative.

We are in a time of asking fundamental questions. What does it mean to be Church today? What do we want our Church to look like today – in my own diocese of Dublin, in Ireland and beyond? What is Christ asking us to be? What is Christ's Spirit inspiring in us? What is holding us back? We have to ask fundamental questions and address them head on.

If we allow ourselves to be led by such questions, we will find ourselves taking a radical look at how we encourage and develop faith in our parishes. We will find ourselves searching for fresh ways to connect the Good News of the Gospel with people's lives. We will find ourselves forming new patterns of working together, both within our parishes and between our parishes.

When I talk about parishes in the future, I speak about "Working Together for Mission". Some think that this is just about different parishes coming together in clusters to meet certain needs. That is only part of the idea. More important, "Working Together for Mission" is about parishes where people work together, where the talents of everyone are fostered in a common mission to see the message of Jesus Christ realised in concrete ways in today's society.

In that way, we will find ourselves learning from one another as we discern the way forward. We will find ourselves becoming heart-driven, inspired by the conviction of each other, as we are touched by the message and teaching of Jesus Christ. Out of this, more and more members of the Church – especially young people

– will discover themselves to be what Pope Francis calls us to be, missionary disciples of Jesus.

This book offers theological reflection that will assist and enrich that process and inspire people in our parishes on their journey together. I welcome this new printing of *Tomorrow's Parish*. Many people in our parishes have already said how helpful the book has been, in putting words on what they experience and in helping shape a way forward. Now this new edition makes that possible for a bigger audience.

Finally, I very much welcome the inclusion of an additional chapter on 'Family', as we journey towards the World Meeting of Families in Dublin in 2018. The vibrancy of tomorrow's parish depends on its embracing young families, in all their different circumstances, so that they come to a deeper delight in the Good News of the Gospel in their midst.

Dr Diarmuid Martin is the Archbishop of Dublin.

INTRODUCTION

The question for tomorrow's parish is not 'how do we survive?' It is 'how do we thrive?' To follow the thread of this second question is to look at ourselves, as parish, in new ways.

Pope Francis has said to 'put all things in a missionary key' – 'to abandon the complacent attitude that says: "We have always done it this way"… to be bold and creative in this task of rethinking' (*The Joy of the Gospel*, 33-34). This book seeks to take up his invitation.

Following the Reformation, a practical part of the Catholic Church's response was to reform the parish system, with defined territories and resident clergy, so that everybody would be cared for. Out of this, the parish came to be what we know it as: an administrative unit within the Church, a structure designed to provide services, a system to be maintained in good working order.

Of course, parish has also meant a sense of community, but this was the kind of structure it became. It was not a missionary period in Europe itself and the parish was not a missionary structure. Diocesan priests were not trained as missionaries, nor did they see themselves as missionaries.

We stand in the shadow of this. We are now locked into this way of seeing 'parish'. We are even weighed down by it. When we think about what is happening with the Church today, we are coming from a mindset that sees the parish as a system of services. Our inclination is to ask 'how can we keep it going?' – 'how can we survive?'

I think that Francis is pointing us in another direction. The challenge is not primarily about how we can restructure our parishes. It is about how we can restructure our minds. It is about thinking of thriving, not surviving.

A sporting analogy: is our present situation more like half-time or more like full-time? There have been some great half-time stories – Liverpool down 3-0 in the 2005 European soccer final; Leinster down 22-6 in the 2011 European rugby final. In each case, something extraordinary happened at half-time. Liverpool went on to win. Leinster went on to win.

Full-time thinking is defeatist. It thinks it is all over. It can only ask the 'survive' question; how can we keep going a little longer? Half-time thinking has a sense of the new. It believes that something new is possible. It thinks of thriving.

When we look around us, at parishes, at people, we can see full-time minds and we can see half-time minds. Francis says to restructure our minds, to see the parish as more than a system to be kept going, to see it in a missionary key, where something new can come to be.

It is already happening in small, but significant ways. People are moving into a missionary mindset. This book is written as a contribution to that movement into 'tomorrow's parish'. The subtitle is 'a vision and a path'. I hope the book helps give shape to the path we are walking, the path we are making.

The first section is about 'situating ourselves'. Parish in a missionary key begins by listening to its context, the situation we find ourselves in today. It listens to what is going on spiritually in people's lives, both inside and outside the faith community. From this situating ourselves comes the call for tomorrow's parish to be a place that both 'reaches out' and 'reaches in'.

The second section – 'rediscovering ourselves' – is about the reaching in. Tomorrow's parish is called to a new sense of what it is to be parish. It sees itself as part of a bigger picture, part of what God is doing in the world. Out of this, a Gospel-inspired vision of parish can be articulated. It is the vision of a faith that is alive and active, at the heart of life. It is the vision of a participative faith community, where previously there was a clerical institution.

A chapter on the 'evangelising parish' brings together these two sections and provides a bridge to the third section. This section – 'expressing ourselves' – is about the reaching out. How the evangelising parish expresses itself is described under four themes. It expresses itself in the practical ways of caring, of welcoming, of listening, of praying. These are primary ways in which tomorrow's parish 'realises' itself as parish.

In this new edition of the book, I have added a further chapter to the third section, on 'Family', for the occasion of the World Meeting of Families in Dublin in 2018. The addition fits in naturally. Family is very much at the heart of the evangelising parish. It will be very much to the fore in tomorrow's parish.

The fourth section is about 'organising ourselves'. This is about mobilising the faith community for its mission. The main focus is on activating the ministry of all the baptised. That is followed by a chapter on building up parish ministry groups. There is a long chapter on the parish pastoral council, the 'engine' of the evangelising parish. The final chapter is about the context of parishes grouping together for mission.

In the course of the book, key characteristics of tomorrow's parish emerge. It will be a community that is itself being evangelised in an ongoing way. It will be a highly participative faith community. It will have a vibrant sense of its mission, reaching out in imitation of Jesus, 'speaking' through its actions even more than through its words.

SECTION A

Situating Ourselves

CHAPTER ONE
Parish Today

If you try to visualise 'the parish', what do you see? What picture comes before you? You might perhaps see a geographical area, though its boundaries may not be that clear to you. Particularly in urban areas, people are less likely to know exactly where one parish ends and the next one begins.

Imagine you are looking down at the parish from above. Some landmarks stand out. You might see the parish church or churches, the parish school, the parish hall or centre, the presbytery or parochial house. So you have a picture of an area, centred on certain buildings where people gather for certain activities (religious and other) or where they come to avail of certain services.

Now ask yourself; who lives in that parish? Here it becomes more complicated. Does the fact that people live in this geographical area – this 'parish' – make them 'parishioners'? The answer, clearly, is no. Somebody might, for instance, belong to another religion, or to none at all. Being a parishioner involves more than just living there. It involves a person's stance towards 'church' and the beliefs it professes, what it stands for.

PARISH AND COMMUNITY

Let us use the word 'community' for the whole population living in the geographical area of the parish. However, it is interesting to note that in Ireland, until recent decades, the words 'parish' and 'community' were almost synonymous. The two overlapped almost to the point of coinciding. It was, to all intents and purposes, a Catholic community and nearly everybody was baptised a member of it. While there were exceptions, they were often not very visible.

So, for example, the parish priest might also have been the chairperson of the local GAA club (the 'parish' GAA club). Or, as has happened, if the same priest wanted to establish a parish council, people might have reacted by saying, 'But we already have a community council; what's the difference?' Parish and community were hard to differentiate.

All this has changed greatly. Part of it has to do with movements of population and new housing developments. This has resulted in a weakening of the old sense of community. Even in rural areas, people say that they no longer know their neighbours. So when I use the word 'community' to refer to the whole population living in the 'parish' area, I am not saying that there is necessarily a strong *feeling* of community.

The other part of what has changed is the relationship between people in the community and 'church'. The number who attend church regularly has declined dramatically over recent decades. Regular churchgoers are more and more a minority. Among those who do not go to church, many remain well disposed and in occasional contact, such as at Christmas, or for a Baptism or First Communion. But many others have left church behind. It is no longer a part of their lives.

This means that we have to see things differently. Maybe we should stop thinking along the lines that 'they are part of our parish'. Maybe we should think instead that 'we are a part of their community'. Thinking 'they are in our parish' could imply that we claim some hold over them, or that they have some obligation to us. Thinking 'we are in their community' implies, rather, that we churchgoers are simply a part – even a small part – of a bigger community.

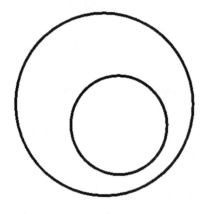

We can put it in a simple diagram. The larger circle represents the community, that is, the population of people living in this particular (parish) area. The smaller circle represents the 'parish'; not in the sense of the area, but that of a subset of the total population or community.

'Parish' may no longer be the best term to use. We might do better to speak of 'the faith community'. This term would refer to the subset of the larger community who identify with church, who see themselves as part of church, who worship in church. Of course, it is not possible to rigidly demarcate who they are. It is too fluid for that. Too many people are tenuously or tentatively connected, maybe 'half in half out'.

BYPASSED

While we cannot rigidly demarcate, we know that the faith community is a decreasing subset of the whole community, a declining percentage of the total. Someone I know offered an image for what is happening that I find quite striking and helpful; the image of the motorway.

Here in Ireland, one thing that was completed before the recession was a good motorway system. When I was young we would go on holidays to Cork each summer. We made our way through Naas, Newbridge, Kildare, Monasterevin, Portlaoise, Durrow, Abbeyleix, Urlingford, Cashel, Cahir, Mitchelstown, Fermoy … It seemed like forever. Since the motorway, I have not been in, or even seen, most of those places. They have been bypassed.

The parish today is like one of those towns or villages. It has been bypassed. It is no longer part of people's journey, no longer on their itinerary. It may be no more than a memory from their past life. Of course, people still come off the motorway if there is something they need; a petrol station or a bathroom or a snack. It is the same with the parish. People will come by for something specific; a funeral, a Baptism, Christmas. But it is usually no more than a detour, sometimes only a once-off.

I began by asking how you would visualise the parish. In what I have said, I have been trying to visualise it somewhat from the perspective of somebody who is not part of it – somebody in the community rather than somebody in the parish. For some people it is in the background, occasionally useful. For others it is just a backwater that is stagnant, irrelevant and useless.

FREEDOM TO CHOOSE

This brings me to speak about the freedom of the parish or, rather, the freedom of the faith community. Freedom is not being able to do just anything we want. The range of what is possible for us to do is circumscribed in all kinds of ways. Freedom, rather, is our capacity to respond to the situation we find ourselves in, whether the situation is to our liking or not.

In exercising its freedom, the faith community can choose to go on as before. It can choose to 'circle the wagons' and close itself off from the outside world. Or, it can attempt to engage with that world, with the community of which it is a subset. The latter is in the spirit of the shift 'from maintenance to mission'. Either can be chosen, inward-looking maintenance or outward-looking mission. Either way it is a choice. In going down the path of maintenance or the path of mission, the parish community is exercising its freedom. It is choosing its future.

I said that freedom is the capacity to respond to the situation we find ourselves in. But the first act of freedom is an act of seeing. The first step is to recognise the situation for what it is. We do not always get even that far. We speak, for instance, of somebody living in a fool's paradise. We talk of people who are in denial. We speak of wishful thinking. These are people who cannot or will not take this first step of seeing well, seeing how things actually are.

This visualisation exercise is the start of seeing the situation for what it is. The next two chapters will take this a little further. Going back to the diagram above, they will look more closely at the two circles. Chapter two will look at the larger circle, to greater discern some of what is going on in the larger community. Chapter three will look at the smaller circle, to reflect on some of what is going on today in the faith community itself.

CHAPTER TWO
'Out There'

The focus of this chapter is the people 'out there' in the wider community. They include people who come to church occasionally, as well as others who come hardly ever. They include people who, though they may have been baptised, no longer profess Christian faith. They include people of different faiths and religions, or those with no religion at all. The specific question I am posing is; what is going on in their lives when it comes to things 'spiritual'?

Think for example of older parishioners talking about their own adult sons and daughters. Frequently, when the topic comes up, they will be heard saying that their children do not go to Mass, but that they are good people. There is a sense of regret, sometimes a sense of failure, about this. And there is also a sense of their sons and daughters, now with families of their own, being wonderful people, with great goodness and deep commitments.

These are the kind of people I am thinking of. It is not some vague category of 'lapsed Catholics'. It is real people. It is younger adults, older adults; single, separated, widowed, straight and gay. What kind of things can we observe about the 'spiritual' dimension of their lives?

We can turn too quickly to questions like, 'how can we get them back to church?' or even, 'how can we reach out to them?'

Maybe we can do nothing until we stop to listen and become aware. Maybe we begin by appreciating. Maybe we begin with the thought that we are on 'holy ground'. Maybe we begin with the thought that God may already be there before us.

The Persistence of the Spiritual

There is a widespread assumption in our society that religion has had its day. In the past it played a central and important role in European culture. It also exercised a great deal of control over people's lives and the workings of society. But that was at a time when, as the saying goes, 'everybody believed except the village atheist'. Belief in God and the afterlife was the 'default' position among the population.[1] Thus, religion or church occupied a central place in society.

Times have changed and things have moved on. The Reformation made for the break-up of Christendom. The rise of science led to the scientific outlook taking hold in society. The growth of capitalism saw commerce displace religion as the 'glue' holding society together. We speak of the 'Enlightenment'. It is a very suggestive word about the emancipation of people and their minds from the control of religion, into ownership of their own powers and potential.

The way people experience the world today – the 'default' – has changed towards unbelief. People still seek the 'fullness of life' Jesus spoke of, but now it tends to be a this-worldly matter. The sense of a before and an after – of a divine creator and a divine afterlife – has receded. The world has moved on, and religion is widely seen as obsolete. Promoting religion can look like trying to sell cassette tapes in the age of the iPod. We live in a secular age.

Even theologians in the 1960s were writing about 'the death of God'. And yet, it seems, God did not die. On the contrary, the last half-century or so has seen the emergence and proliferation of what we loosely call 'spiritualities'. Some of them are focused on a higher being, or a divine energy. Others are nature-centred. Others again are centred on the self. The list is endless, the variety bewildering.

However, to say that religion has had its day does not do justice to the facts (including the fact that it is on the increase in most other parts of the world). It is probably more accurate to say that a certain *kind* of religion is over. This is especially true of the authoritarian, controlling religion that once dominated Europe. With the scientific revolution, we might have thought that the more superstitious forms of religion would also have run their course. But that does not quite seem to be the case.

We are left with the now familiar distinction between 'religion' and 'spirituality'. Religion is commonly thought to refer to the outward, the organised and institutional, with its 'creed, code and cult'. Spirituality is thought to refer to something more inward, the inner journey. The distinction is fine, but it does tend to imply 'spirituality good, religion bad' (an impression greatly accentuated by the abuse scandals).

I recall research done in Britain some years ago, and two of its questions in particular. People were asked, 'do you go to church?' One in eleven said 'yes'. People were asked, 'do you have a spiritual life?' Two in three said 'yes'. This probably captures quite well where we are in Ireland right now. And the point is, going to church is not the same thing as having a spiritual life. To use a familiar phrase, there is much believing without belonging.

European studies over the past few decades echo this. Large numbers of people continue to say that they believe. What it is that they believe in, however, is looser than before. In Ireland,

Micheál Mac Gréil's research covering the thirty or so years up to 2008 paints a similar picture. It confirms the dramatic decline in the numbers going to church. But it also reports that very high numbers still say that they believe in God and continue to pray.[2]

So, a picture is emerging of what is going on 'out there' as regards things spiritual. While church is being bypassed to a great extent, religion in the sense of a spiritual life is far from finished. Something further, something 'more', or beyond, or transcendent, is still part of many people's self-consciousness. It is still a dimension of many people's lives.

It seems though that people continue to value religion. People who do not go to church still want the churchgoers to keep it going! They value its presence and availability, even if only to be accessed occasionally. This has been called 'vicarious religion', meaning religion for the sake of others.[3] But it does mean that events like funerals, Baptisms, First Communion and Confirmation can feel like secular rituals taking place in sacred settings.

BELIEVERS AND NON-BELIEVERS?

I have been talking about 'many' and 'high numbers' of people. But there is a considerable number of others who do not fit into these categories. There are many who have concluded that there is no God and no ultimate purpose to life on earth and nothing after death. When I say 'concluded', I mean that they have re-flected seriously and strenuously on the questions involved.

There are also many who have not given such serious reflection. They live their lives without any apparent reference to God or to anything 'beyond' the day-to-day and the material issues of living. There is little evidence here of a 'spiritual life', though no one knows for sure. Maybe, in some instances, there is something dormant within that the person has lost connection with.

Then there are people who are spiritually lost. Our capitalist-dominated culture is about the immediate, the material. It is about consumption and profit-making. It can be quite unfriendly to the spiritual, except insofar as it has commercial value. The person is treated more as a consumer than as a person. This leaves many feeling deeply uneasy. They sense there is something 'more' – to life; to themselves – but cannot access it.

In all of this, there is something unsatisfactory about the distinction we make between 'believers' and 'non-believers'. To describe somebody as an 'atheist' tells us very little. It is telling us what somebody is *not*. It is not telling us what that person *is*. If somebody says to me, 'I don't believe in God', I am inclined to respond, 'But what do you believe in?' Everybody believes. The question is: what is it that they believe?

The novel *The Life of Pi* offers a wonderful expression of this. The character Pi is a religious person. At college he develops a kinship with one of his lecturers, who is not religious. From this he begins to see that 'atheists are my brothers and sisters of a different faith, and every word they speak speaks of faith. Like me, they go as far as the legs of reason will carry them – and then they leap.'[4]

In this light, the distinction between 'believers' and 'non-believers' looks facile and simplistic. Of course, this explanation will not be acceptable to all. The atheist might not like to be described as a person of faith. Yet the point stands. None of us knows for sure, none of us fully understands. We all make sense, as best we can, of our experience of life. We all come to our convictions and commitments. We all take a leap.

There are also unbelievers who would even use the word 'religious' about themselves. Einstein said that he did not believe in a personal God, but that he was not an atheist. He spoke of his admiration for the structure of the universe, the sense of it being almost too marvellous to comprehend. He spoke of this as a 'religious' attitude to the world. In this use of words, there is a sense that belief in God may be but one form of a religious outlook on life.

A Common Denominator?

I am trying to articulate something that we all have in common, by virtue of our common humanity. It would be good to have a word for this, a kind of 'common denominator'. We could use the word 'faith', or the word 'spirituality'. But the connotations are too strong for many. At the same time, these words are trying to get at something, to articulate something that is an aspect of us all.

Maybe the language of morality and values might work. Think about the following question: Which is deeper, more fundamental in the human person; morality or religion? Most people's immediate answer would be to say morality is deeper. What people mean, I think, is that there is something intrinsic to us about how we live our lives and how we respond to one another. This something has depth; it is about deep meaning, about values. It goes to the core of what we are as human beings.

I would say that there is something very 'spiritual' about this. What I mean is that it has *depth*. Some people's philosophy of life is 'eat, drink and be merry, for tomorrow we die'. But it does not do justice to how we see ourselves. There is something deeper to us as human beings. That is what we believe. And it is independent of whether or not we believe in God.

In this sense I think of true atheists not as people who argue that they are right, but more as people who hope that they are wrong. They are people who are living life at depth, living with integrity, living lives committed to deep meanings and values. Because of this, they feel great frustration that what they hold deepest and dearest will not, as far as they can see, endure beyond this life.

In trying to tease out this depth-dimension that is common to us all, one writer formulated what she called 'seven fundamental aspects of our life experience'.[5] It is very much in the spirit of what I am working on here in trying to articulate a common denominator.

Her seven aspects are:

- ❖ We feel a sense of awe about our life on this planet, and about the highs and lows of human existence.
- ❖ We search for meaning and for connection.
- ❖ We long for a depth of experience, where we are fully alive.
- ❖ We seek the honesty and courage to face life squarely, with its joy and its tragedy.
- ❖ We hope to develop the insight to live wisely.
- ❖ We come to recognise our frailty and shortcomings, especially how we cause fellow human beings to suffer.
- ❖ We struggle to acknowledge our fragility, that we age and suffer and die, and the radical uncertainty this carries.

Here we have the beginnings of a shared language expressing the significance and depth of our human existence. When I spoke about spirituality apart from religion, this is what I was working towards. It is not just that many people believe in God without going to church. It is that a great many people, whether or not they believe in God, are engaged with these issues. It is that a great many are living life at depth. This is what matters in life.

A Different Perspective

From the point of view of church, this new outlook invites us to see things in a different way than before. Let me explain this in terms of three different perspectives.

First, an older way of seeing things was church-centred. Its most notorious expression was in the phrase 'outside the church there is no salvation'. Church, with its sacraments, was where people could access God and find salvation. It was the place where meaning was to be found. Those entering into the church submitted to its teaching, its rules, its way of seeing and its way of behaving.

Second, a newer way of seeing things is God-centred. It sees that God is bigger than church, that God is present through the whole of life, that God is accessible outside of church. And if God is thus, then salvation is also available outside of church. People experience God's liberating, saving presence in all kinds of ways. This the church itself now freely acknowledges.[6] Many who do not subscribe to church would go along with this way of thinking.

But our discussion points to a further, third way of seeing things. In the absence of a shared language, let us call it 'meaning-centred'. People are leading deep, meaningful lives away from religion; but also away from any sense of God, and without reference to God. These people are in touch with – and living from – the depths of their humanity. They do not submit to a meaning supplied by religion, but they have come to find meaning nonetheless.

While God language is acceptable to many who are outside church, speaking in terms of meaning is more universally acceptable. It includes the many who do not see their life's journey in terms of any God. They too are acknowledged by the church. They are described as experiencing God's Spirit, even if that is not how they would describe it themselves.

It all amounts to a very new configuration. I will express it, perhaps crudely, in commercial terms. Let us imagine people as consumers. People are searching. They are 'shopping' for meaning, for depth, for fullness of life. But the church is no longer the only shop in town. Church or religion does not have a monopoly on meaning.

And people look on each 'shop' with the same eyes. They ask; what's in it for me? What is there here that I will find useful? We only need look back on the seven fundamental aspects of life to see what people are searching for. People look at church as they do at any other potential source of meaning – they want to know how it might be of help to them with these issues.

People in the church may see the issue as being just about going to church. But for people 'out there' what matters is not going to church, but living life at depth, living a life that is fully human. There are people who do so live, and people who do not – both among those who go to church and those who do not.

TWO TYPES

The final part of this chapter looks at two types of people. One represents people who are searching for God in new ways after leaving religious practice. The other represents people who may be coming to God for the first time. I imagine that there are a significant number of people who would find that one or the other resonates with their own life experience.

Anatheism

The first type is given expression in the recent book *Anatheism* by the Irish philosopher Richard Kearney.[7] The book is about faith in God in a post-religious world, a secular age. The word he coins for the title begins with the Greek preposition *ana*. It can be defined as: up, back, again, anew. This makes for a thought-provoking set of terms; theism, a-theism, an-atheism, ana-theism.

Thus the book's subtitle, 'Returning to God after God'. Just as, in recent centuries, theism leads into atheism, so there is a third possibility that is neither of these. It is not a return to the previous belief, but is itself a new faith. It is about the God who comes after God. It is a faith beyond faith.

In our post-religious world, many people have rejected 'God'. But it is often unclear just what it is that has been rejected. Is it God? Is it religion? If we read the work of militant atheists, the rejection of God often comes across more as a rejection of religion, particularly its more inadequate manifestations. What I am saying is that, when people reject God, it may well be God as portrayed by religion. It may well be a particular representation of 'God'.

Kearney speaks of the traditional God of religion; all-powerful, domineering, exclusivist, patriarchal, and so on. This God has certainly been widely rejected. The resultant stance is called 'atheism'. But, as should be clear, there may be more to it. It may be not so much that 'God is dead' as that a way of thinking about God is no longer of service to people.

Thus, thinking about God may continue beyond theism in this sense. And while it can lead to atheism, the search can continue beyond atheism too. People can now find themselves in a free space – a space which we can be thankful to atheism for creating. They can find themselves in a space where they can explore anew and choose again, to believe or not to believe.

There is, then, a dynamic of letting go of God in order to lay hold of God; of getting rid of God in order to find God. Kearney plays with the French word *adieu*. He speaks of a goodbye to God; then of a goodbye to the goodbye. There can be a 'to God' (*a-dieu*), a returning (*ana*). But it is not a return simply to what was left behind, to 'theism', to God in the traditional way of thinking. It may be more like finding God for the first time.

This illustrates one type of person; one who, in a post-religious world, has left their religion and its God, and whose journey has brought them beyond atheism to a new sense of 'God' and faith. What comes of it will be very varied, compared to the uniform faith of the past. It may or may not have anything to do with church.

Etty

The second type – about coming to God for the first time – finds expression in the diaries of Etty Hillesum.[8] Etty was a Dutch Jewish woman living in Nazi-occupied Amsterdam. Her diary extends over two and a half years in the early 1940s. She lived in the same city as Anne Frank (and both wrote diaries), but she is not nearly so famous. Her story, however, is in many ways more remarkable.

She began to write a diary in March 1941, when she was

twenty-seven years old. At first it is about her own personal life and her own personal search. But it gradually evolves into a spiritual journey. As the months pass, the Nazi threat comes to centre stage. Jewish freedoms are, bit by bit, whittled away. By mid-1942 Jews are being taken by the trainload to Westerbork, a transit camp north-east of the city, en route to concentration camps in Germany or Poland.

Etty was a Jew, but there is no evidence of any religious upbringing or practice. The diary sees her embarking on a spiritual journey. But because of her upbringing, she is working it out without any prior religious language to help her articulate or name what is happening. She finds herself on a spiritual path, but she is on her own, without the resources religion can offer.

At first, that path is very much about herself, as she moves from a disorganised and wild life to sorting out 'Who am I?' But quite soon the language becomes spiritual. She begins to talk about 'God'. Perhaps most strikingly, she repeats a phrase about 'the girl who could not kneel'. The phrase refers to a desire, an impulse to kneel. Initially she is embarrassed about it, but it becomes the most intimate part of her life. It symbolises her new-found relationship with God.

In mid-1942 she writes, 'There is a vast silence in me that continues to grow.' Through an older spiritual mentor and close companion, she is introduced to Christian literature. She reads Matthew's Gospel, Augustine, Eckhart. She also treasures Rilke's *Book of Hours*. These readings are resources for her search, helping her explore her spiritual self.

From that time, her life revolves around Westerbork. She is part of a Jewish Council of helpers at the camp, until she herself is sent to Auschwitz and death in November 1943. Her last year and a half is characterised by a remarkable other-centredness. As people around her struggle with the awfulness of what is happening, her presence is one of pure help, generosity and support. And, as comes across repeatedly, her base was a deep gratitude for the goodness of life. Amazingly, as conditions grow more terrible, her gratitude grows stronger.

Etty is a gifted writer. Early in the diary she talks of always looking for 'a few words' with which she might capture life's meaning. The thought recurs throughout her writing. Towards the end, speaking to God, she sees her life as 'one great dialogue with you'. It is no longer a few words; now there is just one. 'God'.

Etty illustrates the second 'type'. She stands for those who, in a post-religious world, have not had a religious background, but who have stumbled upon the spiritual path. She stands for those who search, but without the resources such a background might have equipped them with. Here again we can see the great variety in the kind of spirituality that emerges in the modern world. In her case, there is a striking convergence of other-centred living and finding God.

A CHALLENGE

We see a great deal of spiritual living in today's world that is not connected to religion and church. Some of it is Christianity without church. Some of it is God without Christianity. Some of it is a sense of a 'more' without a sense of 'God'. Some of it is people living at depth, their lives imbued with meaning and values. When so much of life today is shallow, ephemeral, self-referenced, it should be a cause of rejoicing that so many are travelling these journeys of faith outside the institutions of religion.

Teilhard de Chardin, the Jesuit scientist and theologian, said that we are not human beings who have occasional spiritual experiences, but rather we are spiritual beings who are having a human experience. What is happening in today's world supports his view. The persistence of the spiritual is testament to the fact that we are spiritual beings. People in the church should be positive in acknowledging these workings of God's Spirit outside of religion.

It means that there is a point of contact with people. But the persistence of the spiritual is also a huge challenge, maybe greater than the challenge of our secular age. It is true that the alternative to religion for many is a pragmatic, this-worldly existence. But for many others, the alternative is that they have found a meaningful life elsewhere. It may be that the institutions of religion are lagging behind people's experience and practice of faith.

This is challenging in the way that competition is challenging. When there is competition, it brings out the best in people. When there are alternative spiritual paths, alternative journeys of faith, the challenge for religion is to listen and to learn; and then to reconnect with its own distinctive riches, and its potential relevance to people's spiritual lives.

CHAPTER THREE
'In Here'

We listen so as to become more aware of our situation. We listen to what is happening 'out there' and to what is happening 'in here'. The interest of this chapter is in what is happening regarding things spiritual within the faith community itself. I am thinking particularly of the local faith community. But the global is also part of the picture. The life of the local faith community is partly conditioned by what is going on in what we call the institutional church.

PROVIDENCE

We begin by acknowledging the most obvious things happening today in the faith community. The following issues come immediately to mind. However, these will not be the direct focus of the discussion.

The numbers coming to church have dwindled. In more and more parishes, those who come to worship could be accommodated by one weekend Mass. By and large it is an ageing population. There are younger people and young families, but the overall impression is one of age. Priests too are getting fewer and growing older. The average age is over 65. How are parishes going to cope?

Recent scandals have led many to dismiss the church as seriously dysfunctional and unworthy of respect. Many within the church, who have a positive experience of their own faith community, also share some of this feeling about the institutional church. Also, predating the scandals, there is a broader credibility problem, illustrated by the church's stance on contraception, its position on homosexuality and its policies about women.

Obviously the church is struggling. It even looks as if it could be on the way out. The 'solution', however, is not to try to put things together again. Imagine if we could get all those people back to Mass. Imagine if the seminaries began to fill again. Imagine if the church's status was restored. That is not what is needed. That would be external change only, bringing the church back to the way things were.

What is needed is a sense of what Christians call 'providence'. Providence is about seeing a way forward in a situation, not a way back. Providence is about omnipresent divine creativity. God is in everything, because God was in the suffering and death of Jesus. This God is a life-giving presence, a God of newness. This God proclaims, 'Do not remember the former things, or consider the things of old. I am about to do a new thing; now it springs forth, do you not perceive it?' (Isaiah 43:18-19).

So it could be that there is a grace in what is happening. Maybe the full churches disguised the shallowness of conformity. Maybe so many priests prevented people taking ownership of their Baptism calling. Maybe the church's standing was cloaking an arrogance and a closedness that can now be confessed. A sense of providence invites us to discern the threads of divine hope that have come out of the situation.

We take hold of hope by delving deeper. We go behind the momentous changes to focus on all things spiritual within the faith community. We pay attention to how we are experiencing 'church'. This is what is meant by things spiritual. It is about how our experience of church has been changing. Naming this change points a way forward.

THE CURVE

The diagram below will help throw light on the situation within the faith community. It comes from Charles Handy, who called it the 'Sigmoid Curve'.[9]

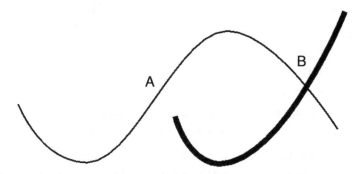

The diagram has many applications. For example, it could be applied to the starting up of a business venture; or to a new parish initiative; or to some phase or project within one's own life. The pattern is often that things take time to get going. There is an initial period of struggle, of investing energy and resources without anything yet to show for it. This is the downward curve. But momentum gathers and things begin to pick up; the curve turns upwards. The business starts to prosper; the initiative starts to bear fruit.

In the natural cycle of things, the project will eventually hit a peak and then go into a phase of decline, a new downward slope. Times change, new circumstances arise, new competitors appear in the market, and there are new needs to be addressed. As the wisdom goes, the time to change is around point 'A' on the diagram. Energy is still high, momentum is strong. But who will listen? 'Why change a winning formula?' 'If it's not broken, don't fix it.' True, and yet...

Often it is when it gets to point 'B' that people start talking about the need to change. The situation is clear, the writing is on the wall. But by this time the energy is gone, momentum is lost and morale is low. Other proverbs now come to mind. 'If you're not moving forward, you're going backwards.'

Now, apply this to the church in Ireland. The highpoint of the first curve was perhaps around 1960 or so. The churches (and the seminaries) were full. Just look at some of the churches built in Dublin about that time. They are huge. If people could have seen twenty years ahead, would they still have built them?

And yet, the early 1960s was also the time of the Second Vatican Council, a convocation of the universal church that was about the church seeing itself in a new way. So at the height of the old curve, a new curve was starting. And it shares the pattern observed in new curves. It takes time to build momentum. It struggles to get going. Decades after Vatican II, where are we now on the new curve? Are we still waiting for it to turn upwards? Or have we reached a point where the new phase begins to take off?

This is very much about how we are experiencing church. There is a sense of living in two churches, one that is slowly dying and another slowly coming to birth. Many people feel part of both, especially if they grew up in the former. Feelings of sadness and hope mingle together; tiredness and energy are found side by side. But it is more than 'either or', either the new curve or the old. It is about carrying forward into the new curve what is of enduring value in the old. That is different to clinging to the past.

With this way of looking at the situation, we can identify both what is 'plus' and what is 'minus' in how we are experiencing church today. This is about internal rather than external factors. 'Plus' refers to what is encouraging in the way we are engaging with the new curve. 'Minus' refers to what is of concern in how we are engaging.

Let us begin with the plus side. The church has been on a new curve since Vatican II and the mid sixties. Looking back over that time, there has been an extraordinary change for the better. I want to describe the change under two headings; as a change in mood and as a change in modes of participation.

A NEW MOOD

First, there has been an extraordinary change of mood. I recall the film *Babette's Feast*, set in a remote Lutheran community in the north of Europe.[10] Their religion is severe, austere, puritanical. Into their midst comes a Parisian woman, Babette, who has lost everything in the French Revolution. She is taken in by two sisters as their cook and servant. (Back in Paris she was a renowned chef in a great restaurant.)

After some time, news comes that she has won the lottery in France. She decides to spend all her money on an extravagant feast of thanksgiving for her new community. The people are taken aback by the lavish preparations and the expensive ingredients being shipped in. With their austere spirituality, they do not know how to react. They have a meeting and come to a decision: we will go to Babette's feast, but will refrain from enjoying ourselves!

The Eucharistic theme comes across powerfully. There is total, unrestrained self-giving. There is a context which expresses celebration and rejoicing. And, as in the Eucharist, there is the transformation in those who participate. We see the initial silence and reserve loosen. People begin to smile and to remember their beginnings. As they remember, they grow in intimacy.

It captures something of the old religion in Ireland, even if it was not quite so severe. Recently, at a parish meeting, one older person talked of when she became a minister of the Eucharist. She was honoured and delighted to be invited. But as she thought of her upcoming first day of duty, she found herself in a quandary. She felt she would like to smile at people as they approached her. But, as she thought more about it, she decided it would not be right.

The mood then was one of duty. Think of the phrase 'Sunday obligation'; such inappropriate language for the celebration of the Eucharist! The vocabulary was that of duty and obligation, obedience and conformity, fear and guilt and punishment. It was as if each of us was shadowed by a cloud of guilt. Sin loomed larger than grace. The message was clear – that our inner selves could not be trusted.

On the new curve, this mood has given way to something far brighter. Most people have now made the transition in their hearts from a God of fear to a God of love; from the doom and judgement of John the Baptist to the Good News of Jesus of Nazareth. Back then Christianity felt more like a religion of bad news and dire warnings. Now the mood is joy. The title of perhaps the greatest document of Vatican II is 'Joy and Hope'. Christianity is to be enjoyed and rejoiced in. A momentous change of mood has come about in a relatively short period of time.

New Modes of Participation

Second, there has been a no less extraordinary change in the mode of participation. We observe it in the space and in the language of the church. The older churches were long, the sanctuary separated off by rails, the altar against the back wall, the priest facing away from the congregation, rows and rows of pews. The Mass was in Latin, a language alien to the people. 'Space speaks', they say. This space expressed how the church then understood itself. It was the space and language of a clerical church.

The newer churches are more circular than rectangular. The rails are gone, the altar has moved into the midst of the congregation, the priest faces the people, the language is the people's language. This new space speaks of participation. We are not simply spectators. We are co-celebrants, celebrating Eucharist together. We can engage in a manner not previously possible. The space and language are those of a people's church.

There is something in this about the 'vertical' and 'horizontal' dimensions of how we experience church. The old churches stressed the vertical; our relationship to God was all the focus. The newer space now also stresses the horizontal, the community and the communal dimension of our experience of church. And it is even more than that. The newer space highlights how we experience God in a communal way.

The transformed mode of participation is reflected in a transformation of ministry. Hitherto, ministry was the domain of the clergy. The laity were on the outside looking in. They were the ministered-to. Their involvement in ministry was very limited. I remember my own mother used to help clean the church each week, and my father helped collect and count the money. There were choirs, there were altar servers, but none of it was really ministry. It was 'helping out', helping the priest.

As the new curve got moving this began to change. 'Ministry' became 'ministries'. Around 1980, ministers of the Eucharist were introduced in this country. We also came to have ministers of the Word, liturgy groups, Baptism teams, communications groups, funeral ministry teams, visitation groups, finance committees, care groups, and more. Perhaps most significant was the introduction of parish pastoral councils. These were to share with the priest the overall care and responsibility for the faith community.

Whenever parishes add up all those involved in parish ministries, they are pleasantly surprised at just how many there are. It amounts to an enormous expansion of 'ministry', of participation, in what is a relatively short period of time. And now it is ministry in its own right. It is more than helping the priest. It is an expression of people's own Baptism calling.

Another aspect of participation is what might be called 'critical loyalty'. Blind obedience and unthinking conformity are things of the past. People have begun to realise that it is possible to belong in a more adult way – in a thinking, questioning way. Institutionally, there is still little recognition of this mode of participating. But locally, more and more people are participating in this way. They feel they belong while not having to agree about everything. The pity is that more of those who have left the church behind did not find this.

Sunday

The new mood and the changed modes of participating are cause for rejoicing. There is much to be thankful for in how we are experiencing church today in comparison to the middle of the last century. But there is also a downside to how we are experiencing church today. Here I will reflect on three themes; passivity, privacy and complacency.

To lead into this, I want to reflect on Sunday, on the experience of Sunday Eucharist. I recall some years ago a colleague took on the project of visiting a different church for Mass each Sunday, to form an overall impression. Imagine that person were you, that you travelled about as an observer in search of a pattern in the experience across different churches. What would you conclude?

I imagine that there would be much that is positive and a lot more that is worrying. The quality of what is experienced on Sunday can be very high. By quality I mean two things in particular. One is the sense of togetherness and community. The other is the sense of prayer and prayerfulness.

Many gatherings score highly in relation to these. But a great many occasions fall short. A parish priest spoke recently of his feeling when he came to the altar one Sunday. As he looked down the church, he felt deflated and just wanted to return to the sacristy.

He could feel what the Mass was going to be like. It was going to be routine, predictable, lifeless; not anything like a 'celebration' of the Eucharist. This is far from being an isolated experience. (And it is interesting that priests have such feelings too!)

For a long time younger people have been saying that they find Mass boring. Now we can see that 'boring' does not mean the opposite of 'entertaining'. It is boring in the sense of being lifeless; lifeless rather than life-giving. When people wish for younger people to come back to Mass, we have to ask, 'back to what?' If the older people were themselves young again, how many would go? They would see the lifelessness in what they have become so accustomed to.

It seems that the plus side we talked about has not percolated down as far as it might have. The new mood, and the new modes of participation, have not penetrated into all hearts. I think this has to do with aspects of the old curve, of the old culture, that do not go away quickly because they are so deeply ingrained.

PASSIVITY

One big aspect is the culture of passivity. The clerical church of the past was a 'provided-for' church. At the height of the old curve, in the mid-20th Century, Ireland had huge numbers of priests and nuns and brothers. There were so many that they did all the ministering. The laity (as the very word suggests) were on the receiving end. That was their role, to be the recipients of ministry.

Imagine a family where the children are never asked to do the dishes or clean their rooms. As they grow up, the parents continue to do everything for them. It means that they are being disempowered. They are not being invited to enter into their responsibility. Something along those lines is what came about in the church.

People were conditioned into passivity for generations, and this conditioning does not shift easily. When, in parish after parish, it is remarked how hard it is to get people involved, this is a huge part of the issue. Laity were never supposed to get involved; that was the priest's job. Likewise, they were never supposed to think for themselves. As a consequence, to get involved requires seeing oneself in a quite different way. It is like asking a seventeen-year-old, for the first time ever, to do the dishes!

PRIVACY

Another big aspect is a culture of privacy. It may be an Irish thing, not being expressive or demonstrative. But it is more than that. In the past, the fact that Mass was in Latin discouraged participation. Mass was something the priest did, and the people watched. People dealt with this as best they could. They followed Mass in a missal, or they said the rosary. It all had the effect of pushing participation inwards. Participation was privatised.

So, the culture we have inherited, our conditioning, is to see Mass as a private devotion. It could be described as multiple acts of individual devotion going on in the same space. It is not unlike the cinema. Everybody is focused on the same screen, everybody is watching the same film, but it is a separate event for each. Our conditioning has left us with a weak sense of Mass as something we do together. We are still on the inner journey, the shift of mindset, from 'getting Mass' to 'celebrating the Eucharist'.

One priest tells a story about himself. He used to always go to the big football matches with some friends. But on one occasion tickets were scarce and he had only one ticket for himself. Off he went; the people beside him were talking to each other, so he watched alone. On the way home he reflected; this is the first time I have ever gone to the match on my own, and it is the first time I have spoken with nobody from start to finish. And then another thought came to him. Is that not what going to Mass is like for a lot of people?

COMPLACENCY

All of this – passivity and privacy – lies behind the lifelessness of much Sunday Mass. We were conditioned to be passive and to be individual. And the conditioning lingers, making what goes on unappealing and unattractive to younger generations. But there is a further aspect also, that leaves us ill-equipped to respond to the situation. Besides suffering from passivity and privacy, we also suffer from complacency.

In the Church of the mid-20th Century, everybody went to Mass. Many went out of the pressure to conform. But because everybody went, an inevitable sense of complacency set in. As someone put it, we came to prefer coma to challenge. Instead of being challenged by Jesus' message, we made it comfortable. We grew content. To a great extent, we ended up going through motions that are dull, dead.

When things changed, we were not ready for it. We were not equipped to respond. We were stuck on the first curve. We had no history of trying to connect with people in creative new ways. Our thinking was likely to be along the lines of 'come back to us'. Come back to us, that is, as we are and on our terms – we are not thinking of changing!

This applies to priests as much as to anybody else. On that old curve, priests, for all their exalted status and mystique, were in some ways like functionaries. The organisation's expectations of them were routine, unchallenging. They were just expected to perform certain duties and to keep things running smoothly. This is not to disregard their commitment and care. It is that they were not trained for mission. They were not trained for leading people through change.

BETWEEN TIMES

It seems that 'church' today might well be described as two churches. There is a strong sense of being between times. We find ourselves situated between an older and a newer experience of church. This accounts for the seemingly contradictory aspects that have been outlined. There is a new mood of joy and there are new modes of participation. And alongside this we see passivity, privacy, complacency.

In the same church we have these contrasting experiences of church. What is happening spiritually 'in here' can be seen to revolve around this contrast, this tension. The issue is about the faith community overcoming inertia and connecting anew with its own identity and its own energy. It is about the faith community as a whole coming up to speed with the new experience and practice of faith that has been emerging within the faith community itself.

CHAPTER FOUR
Parish Tomorrow

'Tomorrow' flows from 'today'. A lively awareness of where things are at today will give indications as to how tomorrow's parish is to be shaped. So, what can we garner from the previous chapters' descriptions of the situation 'in here' and 'out there'? What do they indicate to us about the shape and the focus of tomorrow's parish?

TWO FRONTS

Recalling the image of the motorway from chapter one, we see how parish has been 'bypassed' and has become marginal to many people's lives. But the challenge this poses is on two fronts: it is in here and it is out there. Responding on both fronts is the agenda for tomorrow's parish. Let us summarise what has emerged about each.

'Out there' refers to the larger population of which the faith community is a part. It is not sufficient or satisfactory to say that the world out there is secular or godless and that the challenge is to change it. This is only partly true. Many people's idea of fullness of life is confined to the dimensions of this world. But there is much more going on in people's lives.

Chapter two spoke of the persistence of the spiritual. The spiritual quest has not died out, but has diversified. People continue to thirst for something more. People continue to live life at depth, alive to deeper meanings, responsive to deep values. But there are many sources of meaning and value to be found in today's world. Church is but one source among others.

'In here' refers to the faith community itself. However, there is more to this than what immediately comes to mind; clergy and congregations decreasing and ageing; the loss of credibility and relevance. There are things happening at a deeper, spiritual level. Since the middle of the 20th Century, there has been a huge transition towards a new way of seeing ourselves as church, a new way of being church.

Chapter three described the new mood that has been taking hold, and the new modes of participation that are spreading. But because it is a time of transition, there is also a drag from the way things used to be, pulling us back. There is the lifelessness that comes from a residual passivity, a culture of privacy and a sense of complacency. Perhaps those who have left church or are on the fringes see only this. Perhaps they are not aware of the new way of being church that is coming to birth.

OUTREACH AND INREACH

Tomorrow's parish is one that appreciates the challenges of both outreach and inreach. The following image may clarify how the two are linked together. Imagine a book lying on the table. Some of it is sticking out over the edge. If you push the book out a little, and then further again, it will wobble and eventually topple and fall. There is no longer enough of the book on the table to balance it and support it stretching out further.

The book on the table stands for tomorrow's parish. We talk a lot about the need to reach out. But, as depicted in the image, we must think in terms of *both* reaching out *and* reaching in. We reach out to engage with people out there. We reach in to deepen our sense of who we are as a faith community. As with the book, the parish can only reach out insofar as it is reaching in. There has to be a depth of inreach in order to support outreach.

EXPLORE

Tomorrow's parish reaches out and it reaches in. It holds a balance. But not all responses to the situation achieve this balance. Let us describe four options. One is to ignore. Another is to deplore. A third is to restore. And the final one is to explore. Each represents a different balance between outreach and inreach.

There are some who are not thinking about outreach at all. They choose to go on as before. They choose to circle the wagons, as it were. They aspire to no more than an oasis of comfort for themselves. 'It will see us out,' they may think. This is where people choose to ignore what is going on.

Then there are those who choose to deplore. They deplore what is happening out there. They deplore the materialism in today's world. They deplore how people have abandoned their religious practice. And they deplore what is happening within. They deplore the changes in the church. This is all they see.

In both these options, to ignore or to deplore, there is little inclination to reach out. But there is no inreach either. It is complacent – 'as you were'. The problems are seen largely to lie out there. If there were a real interest in reaching in, it would generate a desire to reach out as well. As it is, these two options are heading for slow but sure extinction.

There are also those who do think about outreach, but who think that outreach on its own is enough. It is outreach without inreach.

It sees only one-way traffic. It thinks simply of 'bringing them back' – sometimes for self-centred motives, to make ourselves feel better. It does not see what is spiritually rich in people's lives out there. And it fails to ask, 'back to what?' It fails to see what is deficient or lifeless in here. This option naïvely wants to restore.

The point is that reaching out and reaching in belong together. Somewhere I came across a piece of research about parishes that reach out. It found that the parishes which were most successful in reaching out were the ones that demanded high standards of themselves. This captures it perfectly. Reaching in is itself an outreach. It becomes a witness. We reach out first of all by challenging ourselves. We cannot truly reach out without reaching in.

When inreach and outreach go together, we are no longer trying to restore, or to ignore, or to deplore. We are ready to explore. Tomorrow's faith community is a place of exploration. Reaching out and reaching in explores new depths. It explores new ways of being church. It explores new ways of engaging with others out there. There is a sense of hope in this, a sense of possibility. There is a sense of the creative God, the God who is doing a new thing.

Exploring is unfamiliar. As a faith community, we are not used to having to reach out, especially in a way that is not patronising or condescending, appreciating the spiritual depth already out there without trying to proselytise. Equally, we are not used to having to reach in. We take our beliefs and roots for granted. We must challenge ourselves to engage in a deeper, newer faith.

A TWO-WAY PROCESS

Inreach and outreach work together in a mutual interplay. Reaching out does something to our reaching in, and reaching in does something to our reaching out. It is dynamic, and has the effect of enriching both perspectives. The diagram below is an expression of it.

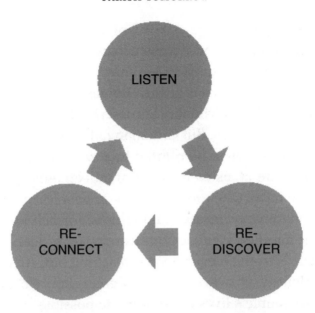

Listen refers to the attitude of the faith community towards the larger community and to what is happening spiritually out there. The faith community listens in an open, appreciative spirit. It appreciates that there is something bigger than church, that God's Spirit is active in all kinds of ways in people's lives. The faith community allows itself to learn, to be enriched, to be challenged.

Re-discover refers to the introspective illumination that listening invites. When we see the diverse ways in which people are living spiritual lives outside of the church, it gives us the possibility of understanding ourselves more clearly. We can come to a sharper, stronger sense of who we are. We can discover what we believe as if for the first time. We can gain new insight into just what we have to offer in a world that is already spiritually rich.

Re-connect refers to the outreach that is built on the foundations of listening and re-discovering. It is a very different way of engaging with people than just trying to 'bring them back'. It respects and learns from where people are in their spiritual lives. It is filled with a new-found amazement at the Good News of the

Gospel. There is now the possibility of a connection between the two – the Good News and people's lives – that people may find creative, relevant, enriching, life-giving.

'Faith comes from what is heard' (Romans 10:17). It is not solely an interior thing. It is spirituality (as described in chapter two) that is interior, intrinsic to us. But Christian faith comes from without, from the other. It has to be offered in a way that is sensitive to where people are at, as well as out of a deep amazement at the Gospel. Then it can take root and grow in peoples' hearts.

It is an ongoing cycle, a spiral perhaps. Inreach and outreach feed off one another. We reach out from an ever-deeper reaching in. We reach in from an ever-deeper reaching out. An ever-richer sense of identity, of who we are, is emerging. An ever-richer relevance to people's lives is being made possible.

The rest of the book will develop this theory further. Section B is devoted to the faith community re-discovering itself, to the bigger picture that gives tomorrow's parish its identity. Section C is devoted to the re-connecting, to the ways in which tomorrow's parish expresses itself, so as to be relevant and life-giving. Section D goes on to discuss how we organise ourselves for this tomorrow.

SECTION B

Rediscovering Ourselves

...ation made it
led to the scienti'

CHAPTER FIVE
The Bigger Picture

The parish is more than just an administrative unit in the church. It is the church in this particular place. It is the local church, the local faith community. Like the whole church, it is not an end in itself. It is not a kind of self-preservation society. It exists to serve a purpose. It is part of something bigger than itself.

When the word 'church' is used in this chapter, it means both the local faith community and the whole church. Either way, it can only understand itself by seeing itself as part of something bigger. It does not find the reason for its existence within itself. It belongs to a bigger picture. Church needs to look beyond, to go beyond, in order to understand itself. The church can be too preoccupied with itself, with its well-being, its expansion, its protection. The parish can be quite inward-looking, seeing little beyond its day-to-day routines, its own little circle of comfort. Centred on ourselves we can, without even realising it, lose sight of that which is our whole reason for existing.

We must stand back and take in the bigger picture. The bigger picture is what gives church and parish their identity. The bigger picture is the reason for which it exists.

This chapter sketches out the bigger picture by reflecting on a series of terms. These terms are: Jesus; Reign of God; Resurrection;

Trinity; Mission; World; and Church. The first six terms represent the bigger picture within which the final term, 'church', makes sense. The following chapters in this section are about how we see the parish in this context.

JESUS

Different people think of different things when they hear the word 'church'. One person thinks of community and a feeling of belonging. Another thinks of institution and authority. Another thinks of prayer and faith. Another thinks of conformity to moral teachings. Another thinks of care. Another thinks of clergy and hierarchy.

But we do not start with the word church. We start with the word Jesus. This is the heart of church, its original inspiration, the source of its distinctive identity. But here too we can ask a question. What do people think of when they hear the word 'Jesus'? As with the word church, people have all kinds of different images.

There are differences, I suspect, between the images held by younger and older people. Christian doctrine speaks of Jesus as fully human and fully divine. That is a hard balance to keep. I imagine younger people would tend more to see Jesus as a great human person. They would find divinity harder to get their heads around. And I imagine older people would tend more to see him as God. They would find the humanity harder to grasp.

It is not surprising, then, that our pictures of Jesus can be unreal. After all, the same figure who weeps at the death of a friend also walks on water! The traditional picture of the Sacred Heart, while it represents a great theological truth, illustrates how unreal our pictures can sometimes be.

A big part of it is the kind of literature the gospels are. They are not reporting facts and events the way a journalist might. They are confessions of faith. The authors want to say to us that

Jesus is the Son of God, our salvation. They want this to come across in everything they write. They are not describing Jesus as he was when they met him. They are describing him from the perspective they came to see him from. They are writing in the light of what they came to see, and that light colours everything.

Scholars today are interested in reconstructing what the historical figure of Jesus was actually like. The distance in time and the genre of the literature mean the results will be limited. The most important recent historical study by John P. Meier is entitled *A Marginal Jew: Rethinking the Historical Jesus*. Jesus was Jewish and he was a marginal figure. He was outside the system. He was not a priest, but a (mere) layperson. He was of humble origins, nobody of consequence.

THE REIGN OF GOD

Jesus says, 'I must proclaim the Good News of the Kingdom of God ... I was sent for this purpose.' (Luke 4:43). Elsewhere, talking of this Kingdom, he says, 'believe in the Good News' (Mark 1:15). This is what Jesus tells us about himself. He tells us that his focus is not on himself, but on the Good News of the advent of God's Kingdom. The word 'kingdom' is his big word. In modern terms it might be termed his calling card, or logo, or brand, or mission statement. Kingdom is his vision and inspiration. It is the passion that absorbs him and drives him.

Kingdom, though, is an outdated word for us. A contemporary translation might be the reign of God. Still, will anybody ever know exactly what he meant by the word? He gives no precise definition. Rather, he speaks of it in a poetic way, with parables. He speaks to the imagination, seeking to evoke a sense of what he means. This itself tells us that what he is talking about is not alien or strange. What he means by God's reign can resonate with something deep within us.

He does not mean a political kingdom. The word 'heaven' might be nearer to it, depending on what we mean by heaven. Sometimes we mean afterlife; but other times we talk about 'Heaven on Earth'. Jesus means both. He talks of the reign of God as 'not yet': 'Your Kingdom come' (Luke 11:2). And he talks of it as if it were already here: 'the Kingdom of God is among you' (Luke 17:21).

The reign of God is perhaps best described simply as what God wants – what God passionately desires for God's people and God's world. The following passage from R.S. Thomas' poem 'The Kingdom' is as good an articulation as I have come across;

> It's a long way off but inside it
> There are quite different things going on:
> Festivals at which the poor man
> Is king and the consumptive is
> Healed; mirrors in which the blind look
> At themselves and love looks at them
> Back; and industry is for mending
> The bent bones and the minds fractured
> By life.[11]

This vision is not 'religious' in the churchy sense of the word. The vision is very much about real life. But it is religious in that it is God's passion. In this same way, Jesus is religious, not in a *churchy* sense, but because he is caught up in God's passion. This is at least part of the significance of his times of intense prayer, as described in the gospels. These are his times of intimate communion with the one he calls *Abba* (Father), when his heart is filled with God's own feelings.

When Jesus says he wants to 'proclaim' the reign of God, it could sound as if he wants to address people. And indeed words are a big part of it. But an even bigger part of it is action. Most of his attention is taken up by people who are sick, people who are poor, people who are excluded. He is filled with God's own compassion for them. Compassion is a strong word in the gospels. It means feeling the pain of another as if it were one's own. When people encounter Jesus, they experience the compassionate face of God. They experience the reign of God.

But Jesus does not stop at compassion. His compassion is accompanied by criticism. It leads him to name and to criticise the reasons why people suffer. It brings him into conflict with the religious authorities, whose dismissive treatment of people reflects a dismissive, exclusive God. The conflict escalates and eventually leads to his execution. He dies for what he believes in.

RESURRECTION

What comes next is represented by a remarkable turnaround. People along the way had been drawn to Jesus with different degrees of intensity. There were the crowds who followed him at various places. There were more long-term companions, or disciples. And then there were the twelve, his inner circle as it were. With his death, almost all of his closest companions scattered in fear and disillusion. Yet hardly had they gone when they gathered again, this time in joy and amazement. The reason is: Jesus risen.

The word 'church' originally meant just this. It meant people who were 'gathered', gathered because of Jesus risen. When we say 'risen' we are not talking of resuscitation; that would just mean 'he lives again'. Resurrection means transformation, a transformed presence. Jesus, in death, has entered into a new sphere of existence. The New Testament speaks of it as his being 'seated at the right hand of the Father'. Jesus is present to them from there. They experience the real presence of Jesus transformed. This is what gathers them.

One of the earliest faith-confessions of the regathered companions said simply, 'Jesus is Lord.' The proclaimer had become the proclaimed. The one who proclaimed the reign of God is now himself proclaimed as Lord. Resurrection means that the vision he proclaimed did not die, but lives with him and through him and in him. The Good News he proclaimed is real. He himself is the pledge. He himself is its heart. He himself is the Good News.

This marks a culminating point. Individual men and women had come into contact with Jesus of Nazareth. As they got to know him they became captivated. Peter says to Jesus, 'Lord, to whom can we go? You have the words of eternal life' (John 6:68). They sense a 'more' to him, 'Who then is this, that even the wind and the sea obey him?' (Mark 4:41). The resurrection is the culminating point in the relationship. It is the revelation of who he is. This is captured, for instance, in their confession, 'In him all the fullness of God was pleased to dwell' (Colossians 1:19). They confess that, in him, humanity and divinity are one.

TRINITY

Pithy confessions, such as that above, capture something of what the first disciples came to realise about Jesus. The New Testament writings can be seen as an extended reflection, teasing this out, putting words on the experience, unfolding its implications, communicating its hope for the world. This leads the disciples to what would later be called the doctrine of the Trinity.

As the disciples 'process' their experience of the resurrection, they find themselves speaking of 'God' in a threefold way. It is most familiar to us in Paul's farewell greeting to the Christians in Corinth: 'The grace of the Lord Jesus Christ, the love of God, and the Communion of the Holy Spirit be with all of you' (2 Corinthians 13:13). God is no longer just 'God'. God now has a face and a name. In another example, Paul says, 'If the Spirit of him who raised Jesus from the dead dwells in you ...' (Romans 8:11). In one short phrase he mentions the Father, the Son and the Spirit.

Let us not overlook the critical point contained in Paul's last three words, 'If the Spirit of Him who raised Jesus from the dead *dwells in you.*' This talk about God is also talk about us. Listen again to Paul: 'God has sent the Spirit of his Son into our hearts, crying "Abba! Father!"' (Galatians 4:6). It is the same threefold language about God, and again it embraces us. The whole purpose of God in the world, revealed in the risen Jesus, is God's sharing of God's life with humanity.

The word 'Trinity' is not found in the New Testament. This is long before the doctrinal formulations of later centuries. It is very different from theoretical speculation. Here we have people who underwent a remarkable experience and who sought to put words on it. And these three words – Father, Son, and Spirit – are what emerged to articulate their experience of God, as revealed to them in the resurrection.

In the early centuries, especially in the Eastern tradition, the word 'deification' was central. God became human so that we would become divine. This was what salvation, being saved, meant; that we are in process of entering into our divinity. This is the heart of the mystery, the heart of what Christians believe. This is where the disciples' experience brought them. The revelation of who God is is also the revelation of our human destiny; to participate in the very life of God as Father, Son and Spirit. This is the reign of God. It is both already and not yet.

MISSION

This brings us to the word 'mission', and to the original meaning of that word for Christians. Mission means sending, but when we think of the word we rarely have its original meaning in mind. We may think of 'the foreign missions', going back to the European conquests and colonisations of the 16th Century and after. We may think of the old-style parish mission. We may think of the talk of shifting 'from maintenance to mission' in pastoral strategy. But originally, mission was none of these.

Before the 1500s, before the foreign missions, mission was an important word in theology. The word referred to God. Mission means sending, but it also implies movement. It refers to the movement *within* God, the dynamic interplay of love between Father, Son and Spirit. And it referred to movement *outside* God, the movement of God towards God's creation.

Primarily, mission is not about us at all. It is not about our being sent. It is God's movement towards humanity. John's Gospel is an extended illustration of this, with its repeated use of the word 'send'. Again and again, Jesus talks of 'the one who sent me'. At the Last Supper he talks of sending the Spirit. And in his risen presence he says, 'As the Father has sent me, so I send you' (John 20:21). When we think of mission, we are to think of something that God is doing. Mission is God's reaching out so that all might share in God's life.

WORLD

Next, this understanding of the divine mission tells us the meaning of the world we live in. The world, as we know, is an ambiguous place, where great good and great evil live side by side. Sometimes religion sees the world as a place of sin (in contrast to church, being the place of grace). But in the bigger picture, as sketched here, that is not quite how it ought to be seen.

Here, the world is simply the object of God's love. In the words of John's Gospel, 'God so loved the world' (3:16). And God has been loving the world since the beginning. The 'big bang' was God setting in train the whole evolutionary process. That process is the unfolding story of God's love for the world, God's mission towards the world.

The world, for all its ambiguity, is God's project. It is God's 'work-in-progress'. The world is imagined by God, brought into existence by God's love. Its unfolding story is accompanied by God, imbued with God's Spirit in its 'groaning in labour pains' (Romans 8:22), its process of self-realisation, its process of becoming itself.

So the world is not a passing phase on the way to something better. It is where the reign of God is already taking shape. Vatican II echoes Jesus' own vision: 'it is here that the body of a new human family grows ... Here on Earth the Kingdom is mysteriously present.'[12] The reign of God is God's future for the world, its ultimate transformation, a 'new Heaven and a new Earth' (Revelation 21:1).

This is the Good News of Christianity, this Good News about the world. The Incarnation began, not 2,000 years ago, but 14 billion years ago with the origins of the world. What happened 2,000 years ago is the culminating point. The resurrection of Jesus brings to light how the story of the world is the story of salvation. But the story of salvation begins in creation. It is the story of God loving the world into being for its inexpressible future.

CHURCH

It is only now that we can really speak about church, only in the context of this bigger picture. It is true that church is sent, called to mission in the world. But saying that could give the impression that mission is something devised by the church, which it then embarks on. It could give the impression that church comes first, mission after. It could lead us to think that church comes first, then the world.

But it is the other way around. Mission leads to church, not church to mission. Mission is God's movement towards the world and humanity. 'Trinity' means a missionary God, a God who is reaching out to humanity and to all God's creation. And from this, 'church' is born, caught up as a partner in God's mission.

Church is born out of the outpouring of God's Spirit in the world. Vatican II put it succinctly, saying that the church 'is by its very nature missionary since … it has its origin in the mission of the Son and the Holy Spirit.'[13] Church exists so as to be the continuing mission of Jesus in the world, in the power of the Spirit. Its mission is the divine mission. This is the 'something bigger', the bigger picture wherein church can begin to understand its own self.

The church is at the service of this bigger picture. It is sent for this process of the world becoming itself, the world being transformed into God's reign. That process is what matters, the process of God's work-in-progress. Church itself is not the process, but a presence, a dimension, a help. The process is bigger than church and is going on in all kinds of ways – and places – apart from church.

The church does not 'bring' salvation to the world. Salvation is the story of God's creating us and loving us, the story of our deification, the story of the transformation of the world. The world is where salvation is happening. That is not the language used by the world, that is the language church can offer. Church, in this perspective, is the place of revelation, the visible sign of God's reign. It is the place where the meaning of what is going on in the world has come to revelation.

I think here of the image of the keys which Jesus gives to Peter. Keys can be for letting people in. If I hold the keys, I decide who gets in and who does not. But keys can also be for unlocking; unlocking what was hidden, bringing to light what was obscure. An image of power and an image of service. We ought to think of the church in the second sense rather than the first. The church's presence brings to light what was obscure. It unlocks the meaning of the world for the world.

This way of seeing church and world gives a perspective on what was discussed in chapter two, about what is happening regarding things spiritual outside of church. We spoke of spirituality apart from religion, of people living life at depth. We can now see this as God's Spirit, God's grace manifest in God's world. This is God's work-in-progress. This is God's saving presence in the lives of God's people.

IDEAL AND REALITY

What has been sketched above is the ideal. But there is always a tension between the ideal and the reality. So let us sketch a little of how the reality falls short. The dynamics involved are typical of organisations in general, not just the church.

In the early stages, the ideal is strong. The original prophetic figure and the originating vision are inspirational. A community forms and the vision pulses through its members. There is an outward thrust, an impulse to share what has been experienced. It is a mission.

Then reality sets in. There is need for organisation and a concern for structure, especially as numbers multiply. Attention is deflected inwards. The organisation is increasingly preoccupied with its own maintenance, with maintaining the operation. Issues of power and control come to the fore. With success, complacency sets in. Things are just ticking over. There is no urgency. There is no listening to any challenging feedback.

By way of illustration; at a gathering some time back, the speaker arrived with a very large, pot-bound plant. As it stood prominently on the table, all could see how the roots were curling around and how the plant had become tangled up in itself. He brought it, he said, as a symbol for our church today. We can see how the pot-bound plant symbolises a church that is inward-looking, institutionalised, complacent.

There can then be a movement for reform in response to the need for space, for air, for light. There is a newly awakened sense of the originating vision. There is a desire to re-connect, to be revitalised. And so it becomes an ongoing tension – the new life and the dead weight, the inspirational and the institutional, the energy and the complacency. Church is meant to be in perpetual reform, permanent revolution.

It has been described as a tension between a church-centred mission and a mission-centred church. A church-centred mission means a self-centred church, a church concerned with itself, with its growth or aggrandisement or power. A mission-centred church is God-centred and world-centred. What matters is not church but God. What matters is the bigger picture of what God is doing in the world, through Christ in the power of the Spirit. When people see church, it is this that they are meant to see.

The bigger picture is what makes sense of church. It is where church makes sense of itself. This has been the theme of the chapter. But what is said of church is also to be said of parish. Now it is time to discuss parish in terms of the bigger picture, to articulate a vision of parish.

CHAPTER SIX
A Vision of Parish

There is a story about tourists in a great city. They come across a huge building site but can find no sign to indicate what is going on. They see some stonemasons at work and approach them. They inquire of the first what they are doing. 'We're cutting stones,' he replies. They move on to the second. 'We're earning one hundred euro a day,' he says. They ask the third stonemason the same question and he answers, 'We're building a cathedral.'

Three answers to the same question. Let us ask the same question in the parish. We go among those involved in different parish activities or ministries and ask 'what are you doing?' The answers might be along the following lines: 'I read at Mass;' 'I clean the church;' 'I help with the funerals;' 'I sing in the choir;' 'I manage the website.' It all sounds very like the first stonemason.

That is as we would expect. But it would be great to have more conversation along the lines of the 'cathedral' answer. It would be great if people described not just what they are doing specifically, but what everyone is contributing to. What is it that we are all working towards? What is the 'cathedral' we are building? What is the 'jigsaw' we are all pieces of? What is the heart of 'parish'? What is our shared passion? What is the vision that inspires us? The answer is somewhere within us, but just has not been brought to the surface.

This is all very much related to the 'bigger picture' of the last chapter. This chapter is about the bigger picture as applied to the parish. It is about parish re-connecting with its bigger picture, bringing it to light. To this end, I will first reflect on what three recent popes have said about our vision of parish. Then I will relate what they say to a Gospel perspective. Finally, I will put their reflections in conversation with the bigger picture; what they see happening in the parish and what is happening in the gospels.

The reflections are very brief. One is a talk given by Paul VI in 1963. One comes twenty-five years later, from a document of John Paul II. The last is twenty-five years later again, from Francis. These three passages, spanning the last half-century, have a great deal to offer by way of putting words on what our 'cathedral' is.[14]

PARISH *IS* CHURCH

Early in his reflection, John Paul II speaks about what the parish is *not*. 'The parish is not principally a structure, a territory, or a building.' Francis says it is 'not an outdated institution'. He expresses his concern that it 'not become a useless structure out of touch with people or a self-absorbed cluster made up of a chosen few'. And he recognises the challenge we face today when he comments that the effort to renew our parishes 'has not yet sufficed'.

There is a strong sense here of needing to connect with something bigger. Indeed, the word 'parish' may itself be a difficulty. It is not an exciting word, it is quite ordinary, even bland. It does suggest territory, buildings, structures, institution. It may even suggest 'out of touch' or 'self-absorbed'. The word may suggest something much less than what parish is meant to be, as these quotations testify.

And yet, there has been a revolution going on in how we think about parish. It goes back to the Vatican Council in the 1960s, when the church was starting to reflect and see itself in a new way. We are more than an institution, more than a hierarchy, more than a highly centralised, controlling multinational organisation. We are God's people, the Christian community.

All this applies to parish as well as to church. Parish is more than an administrative unit. It is more than a local branch office of a big organisation, administered by its officials, its clergy. It is more than a place to go to avail of the organisation's services. Yet this is how it can be seen, not just from the outside, but also among those who are on the inside.

Parish personnel are often frustrated by the way that baptised people who do not frequent church come on occasion to use its facilities, such as for funerals and baptisms. But also, people who *do* frequent the liturgies and activities of the parish can look on parish as simply a service that is provided for them by the clergy. Indeed, on the analogy of the local branch office, it may not even matter which branch, which parish, they go to, as long as the service is available to them.

In trying to connect with a bigger picture, John Paul II brings the words church and parish close together. His perspective is quite different from the mentality of institution and branch office. Parish, he says, is where 'the church is seen locally'. It is 'the place where the very "mystery" of the church is present and at work'. In the same way, Francis says that the parish 'is the presence of the church in a given territory'.

In terms familiar to us, the global is local. The greatest self-expression of 'church', its highest act, is when it celebrates the Eucharist. Yet Eucharist can only be in a particular place. So, when the local Christian community gathers for Eucharist, everything that 'church' is is there. This is much more than a branch office. A branch can be shut down; the organisation at large is all that matters. So it is in this sense John Paul II calls the parish a 'Eucharistic community'.

This is why everything said about church in the last chapter is to be said about parish also. Parish *is* church in this particular place. It takes its identity from the bigger picture it is a part of. It only understands itself when it looks beyond, to something greater than itself. The divine mission tells the parish what it is. God's outreach to humanity in the Son and the Spirit is what matters. Church, parish, is about the 'today' of that outreach.

MISSION-ORIENTED

Because parish *is* church, it is no surprise that the three popes see it in the context of mission. In putting words on what the 'cathedral' is, Paul VI, John Paul II and Francis all speak about mission. Paul VI says, 'We believe simply that this old and venerable structure of the parish has an indispensable mission of great contemporary importance.' It is a striking juxtaposition. 'Old', 'structure'; that is what many would associate with 'parish'. But it is more. It is mission. It is indispensable. It is contemporary.

John Paul II talks of 'its fundamental vocation and mission'. Francis describes it as 'a centre of constant missionary outreach', called to become 'completely mission-oriented'. Mission-oriented is the opposite of what Francis calls a 'self-absorbed' parish. It reflects a parish that is in touch with its identity, the something bigger than itself.

Community

The meaning of mission can be teased out through a number of important themes in the documents. The first of these is community. Paul VI says that the mission is firstly 'to create the basic community of the Christian people'. John Paul II describes the parish as 'the family of God, a fellowship afire with a unifying Spirit, a familial and welcoming home, the community of the faithful'. Francis calls it 'a community of communities', an environment of 'living communion and participation'.

The word 'participation' is really worth highlighting here. When parish is seen as a clerical institution, people are passive, submissive, provided for. But community is participative and collaborative. John Paul II emphasises the participation of all in parish life. He talks of how each Christian is 'unique and irreplaceable'. Each one is 'called by name' and 'entrusted with a unique task which cannot be done by another'. He talks of 'the missionary effort of each'. In the same spirit, Francis says that all members are 'to be evangelisers'.

I would also highlight the theme of welcome. For John Paul II, the mission is 'to be a place … to gather … to be a house of welcome to all and a place of service to all.' The other words he uses – 'family' and 'home' – convey the same mood of welcome. A place of welcome has the feeling of openness and generosity of spirit. It evokes hospitality, belonging, acceptance and inclusion. It is a whole way of being parish.

Connection

A second theme is connection. A big part of the mission of the parish is about connecting with people. The parish, according to John Paul II, 'is the church placed in the neighbourhoods of humanity'. For Francis, the parish is 'the church living in the midst of the homes of her sons and daughters'. This is about presence. The parish is not cut off from the real world in some 'religious' world of its own. It is present among and for the people of this particular place.

Francis insists that the parish must really be 'in contact with the homes and the lives of its people'. For John Paul II, 'it lives and is at work through being deeply inserted in human society and intimately bound up with its aspirations and its dramatic events'. He goes on to refer to the 'disintegration and dehumanisation' that can affect society, and to how people can be 'lost and disoriented'.

This theme of connection carries a strong tone of sensitivity and care. The parish's presence in the community is a sensitive presence. Sensitive means the opposite of numb; sensitive means being able to feel. The parish is a community that opens itself and allows itself to be affected by what is going on in people's lives. It is affected by the pain and struggles in people's lives. It is sensitive to people's deepest desires and aspirations.

This sensitivity is what enables the parish to connect with people. Being a welcoming community, it is sensitive to what life can be like for people. When it is such a community it can, in the words of Paul VI, 'put solidarity into practice' and exercise a 'charitable outreach'. Its caring response can make a difference to people in their lives.

Both Francis and John Paul II draw on the image of thirst. The parish can be 'a sanctuary where the thirsty come to drink in the midst of their journey' (Francis). It is like 'the village fountain to which all would have recourse in their thirst' (John Paul II). The thirst may be for meaning and hope; it may be for care and support; it may be for community; it may be for God. When parish welcomes and connects, people can find refreshment for their thirst and support on their journey.

Faith

The third theme is faith. I said earlier that 'faith community' might be a good alternative term for 'parish'. Indeed, the theme of faith brings together some further thoughts from the documents. Parish is where people gather together to celebrate the Eucharist (John Paul II). Part of its role is 'to initiate and gather' people in liturgical celebration (Paul VI). It is 'an environment for hearing God's Word, for … worship and celebration' (Francis).

These thoughts point to faith being a together thing. We are not Christians on our own. We gather. We belong together. The word 'companion' is suggestive here. It literally means 'bread together'. We break bread together – we are companions on a journey. The faith journey is a together journey. In our togetherness, faith is enriched.

Thus, the worshipping community is the place for 'growth in the Christian life' (Francis). It is where people grow in faith. As Paul VI puts it, the mission is 'to support and renew people's faith today'. He calls the parish a 'school for teaching the saving message of Christ'. In celebrating faith, and in nourishing and building faith, the parish community is entering into its deepest identity.

THE GOSPEL PICTURE

These reflections present a picture of parish that goes far beyond the branch office or the administrative unit, the old structure or the outdated institution. Now I wish to put these reflections in conversation with the gospels. I want to compare what happens in the gospels with what these three popes describe as happening in the parish. There are some strong echoes.

Welcome

Today, we appreciate Jesus' practice of table-fellowship as being the very heart of who he was and what he was about. The gospels depict him at meals with various people, including Pharisees. But what stands out, and what gets noticed, are the meals he shared with the ones called 'outcasts' in the gospels. In Matthew, the Pharisees ask his disciples, 'Why does your teacher eat with tax collectors and sinners?' (9:11) In Luke, the Pharisees and scribes 'were grumbling and saying, "This fellow welcomes sinners and eats with them"' (15:2).

These meals were 'Eucharistic'. They were the many suppers he shared before what we call 'the Last Supper'. They are all about what he gave of himself to others – the Eucharistic logic of transformation. 'Outcasts' were people who were out in the cold, judged, ostracised, regarded 'with contempt' (Luke 18:9). What often happens with such people is that they internalise the message. They come to regard themselves with contempt. They lose a sense of their having a future where they can exist as persons.

Jesus' table-fellowship with them was a simple but powerful gesture. It was an experience of welcome, of hospitality, of being accepted and included. It was transformative. The transformation can be seen in the abundant generosity of Zacchaeus (Luke 19). It can be seen in the overflowing love of the woman who bathes Jesus' feet (Luke 7). Love, that previously was blocked up, is released in them. They begin to exist again as persons.

In the story of the woman charged with adultery (John 8), the 'clash of logics' is to the fore. The logic of her accusers is that she is defined by her past. There is no more to her; she may be stoned to death. The logic of Jesus is expressed in his words to her: 'neither do I condemn you. Go your way and from now on do not sin again.' Jesus sees her as future. She is a person and, if a person, then also somebody with a future. Welcome invites people to flourish.

Compassion

The story of the most magnificent meal of all – the feeding of the 5,000 – begins on a note of care. When Jesus saw the crowds 'he had compassion for them' (Matthew 14:14). We have already talked about Jesus' compassion. Like welcome, it is at the heart of who he was. The actual word occurs at key points in the gospels, such as to reinforce its significance. Jesus feels compassion for the widow of Nain (Luke 7), for the leper (Mark 1), for two blind men (Matthew 20). And in his two greatest stories, the Good Samaritan feels compassion for the man lying by the roadside; and the father is moved with compassion for his prodigal son (Luke 10 and 15).

We can think here of Jesus' healings; they add up to a long list. There were people who were blind or deaf or dumb, lepers, people possessed, epileptics, the paralysed. There is a real sense of the years of suffering and unending pain. There is a woman suffering from haemorrhages for twelve years; a man paralysed for thirty-eight years; a boy suffering from epilepsy since childhood; a woman crippled and bent over for eighteen years. Jesus' heart is a heart drawn to suffering. It affects him – he feels it as if it were his own.

Jesus' encounters with people in welcome and care are experienced by them as 'good news'. They hear good news about themselves and good news about God. In the depths of their being they hear that they are loved by God. In Jesus' love, people connect with God's love. So the encounters are encounters of faith. Frequently, Jesus says to the one healed, 'your faith has made you well'. In the presence of Jesus, faith is affirmed and faith grows.

EARTHING THE GOSPEL

Even such a brief reflection shows how the words about parish in the papal documents find a strong echo in the gospels. Maybe it is more of an amplification than an echo! The parish is a participative community. It is home, a place of welcome and inclusion. It seeks to connect with the real lives of people. It is a place of sensitivity, solidarity, care. The parish is where people hear God's Word, a place where faith grows. It is a Eucharistic community, a fellowship gathered around the table of the Lord. The convergence between what happens in the gospels and what is meant to happen in parish is compelling.

This is the bigger picture, the 'cathedral'. What goes on in the gospels is what parishes are called to be. When the parish is as described above, it is the Gospel. It is the Good News being proclaimed. The mission of the parish is to be the 'today' of the Gospel, the today of the resurrection and its transformative power. Parish 'earths' the Gospel. What happened *then* is *now*.

'Do This'

The gospels record two commandments of Jesus at the Last Supper. Matthew, Mark and Luke record his 'Do this in memory of me' as he shares bread and wine. John records his 'You also should do as I have done to you' as he washes the disciples' feet. The two commandments need to be heard together. They do not belong apart. Together they are shorthand for the mission of the faith community, shorthand for what it is meant to be.

When we hear 'do this in memory of me', we might ask, 'do what?' The command may point us to the Eucharist and no more. But if we do only this, then we have only a religion of ritual. 'Do this' should also point us to the washing of feet, the symbolic action that stands for Jesus' way with people, his welcome and his care.

The mission of the parish is to 'do this' in both senses. It is called to gather for the breaking of bread; to hear the Word, to remember and to be re-amazed by the Good News of the Gospel, to feel its connection to life. And from this gathering the faith community is sent; to be what it celebrates, welcoming and connecting and caring. When it 'does this', it participates in the divine mission today. Then the divine mission *is* today.

Real Presence

The same goes for another phrase we use about the Eucharist, the 'real presence' of the risen Lord in the breaking of bread. Just as 'do this' may point to the Eucharist and no more, so we may think of presence as being about the Eucharist only. But again, it is more.

When parish is earthing the Gospel for today, it means that what people are experiencing there is the same as what people experienced in the pages of the gospels. It is the same welcome, the same care. It is the same presence. People are encountering the risen Jesus, really present, not only in the Eucharistic gathering, but also in the daily practice of the Gospel of welcome and care.

Think back to the 'circles' of chapter one. The large one repre-sented the population of the geographical area ('parish'). The smaller one represented the faith community within that larger community. The faith community ('parish' in that sense) is called to be a presence in the larger community. But people can be 'present' in different ways. We can be physically present but not really in touch. We can be preoccupied or self-absorbed. Or we can be 'really' present.

The faith community is really present when it is being true to its mission and calling. Its calling is to 'reach in', to re-amaze itself or allow itself to be re-amazed, as it listens to the Word and gathers for the breaking of bread. It is called to 'reach out', in welcome, in sensitivity and care, to connect with the real lives of people. When this is happening there is a real presence of church in the larger community. And in that there is the real presence of the risen Lord, the Good News of God.

An Experience

What it all comes down to is that parish is not a structure or an institution. It is an *experience*. All the words that we have been using are about an experience. Parish is meant to be an experience of community, of welcome and belonging, of acceptance and inclusion. People are meant to experience a connection, to experience care and solidarity. Parish is a place where people experience refreshment or nourishment for their spiritual thirst. It is an experience of faith. It is an experience of the real presence of the risen Lord.

People 'out there' can come to sense this. They can come to share in the experience. God is already there in their lives. All are already travelling the spiritual journey. But when parish is being what parish is meant to be, people can find in it something very relevant to their journey.

They might find that they are noticed. They might find things being done that show an awareness that they are there. They might experience acts and initiatives of care for themselves, born of this awareness. They might feel a sensitivity to their situation and to what is going on in their lives.

They might also hear a message of welcome. They might find the parish putting itself forward as a place of hospitality. In any dealings they have with the parish, they might also have that experience of being welcomed. They might hear a message of inclusiveness, a message of being respected and affirmed, a message of being accepted without judgment.

Such a parish would appear to people as an outward-looking place, a community with a generous spirit. And, if they came forward to see further inside, they might find a place of life and light. It might be a place where the sense of dull routine is absent, where the people gathered have a vibrant sense of who they are. They would sense a hope alive among them. They might themselves feel a desire to be introduced to the source of that hope.

Home from Home
Our word 'parish' has interesting roots in the New Testament. There, *paroikos* means an exile or a resident alien. And *paroikia* means a stay in a foreign country. Thus the first letter of Peter offers advice on how to live during our time as 'exiles' (1:17; 2:11). Abraham's people lived as resident aliens in the land of Egypt (Acts 7:6; 13:17). Christians are seen as sojourners in this world, dwelling in this place as strangers.

But to this Paul adds the thought that 'you are no longer strangers and aliens, but you are citizens with the saints and also members of the household of God' (Ephesians 2:19). Christians are 'parishioners' in this complex sense. They are at home and they are not at home; both members of God's household and resident aliens. Their true home is elsewhere. They belong to the future, to God's reign. They live out of that future. In an image from Hebrews (6:19), their present lives are 'anchored' in their resurrection hope.

Parish, then, is a 'home from home'. Earthing the Gospel is creating this home from home, this foretaste of what will be. 'Do this in memory' makes the past, the pages of the Gospel, real today. But it also makes the future real. The first letter of John says that 'we have passed from death to life because we love one another' (3:14). We *have* passed. When we 'do this', in the full meaning of Jesus' command, we are already experiencing what is our eternal destiny. The 'big picture' is already taking shape.

CHAPTER SEVEN
A Disciple's Faith

'Faith community' is a good term for parish. This chapter teases out what the word 'faith' means. Parish is a community where faith is awakened, enriched, nourished, supported and deepened. But faith community is more than just another term instead of parish. It is more than a description; it is an aspiration. It is what the parish wants to become, a community that is growing in faith.

But what exactly is the parish hoping for? What does this faith look like, the faith it nourishes? The focus here is on the individual person, the faith of each member of the community. Here we are applying the 'bigger picture' to the individual. Growing in faith, and as members of the faith community, we grow into the bigger picture – the bigger picture that church is all about.

The language we use leaves something to be desired. What do we call ourselves as individual people of faith? We call ourselves 'Catholics', or 'parishioners', or 'lay people'. It is not strong language. It does not communicate much about the goal, the aspiration. A Catholic or a parishioner is what I *am*. But what am I *becoming*? What is the faith that I am aspiring to? Faith is not something static, something I either have or do not have. Faith is a process, a journey, a task, a challenge, a becoming.

The word 'Christian' is stronger. It has a sense of a calling and it has a sense of becoming. The parish is a community of disciples. I think the word 'disciple' is as good a word as there is, even if it is not part of ordinary discourse. A 'disciple' is a follower. The word means somebody who has chosen. A disciple is resolute, is committed, on a journey, growing into discipleship.

It is not only the language that can fall short, but also the reality. Here we may observe the different forms that a 'weak' faith takes. Faith can be on a tangent to a person's real concerns. It can be in a compartment of its own, with little or no connection to other parts of life, such as family or work. Maybe it comes into play only occasionally. Maybe it is unsure of itself.

Chapter three referred to other weak forms of faith. There is faith that is private, 'for me', with little interest in a community of faith. There is faith that is passive, happy to avail of services provided by others, wanting no further involvement. There is a faith that is complacent, stuck in routine, institutionalised, comfortable. There is what one theologian speaks of as a merely 'believed-in faith'.

> Are we living as disciples, or do we just believe in discipleship and, under the cloak of this belief in discipleship, continue in … the same unchanging ways? Do we show real love, or do we just believe in love and under the cloak of belief in love remain the same egoists and conformists we have always been?[15]

What follows will tease out what the 'end product' looks like, when faith becomes all it can be. Earlier I mentioned research which indicated that the parishes that are successful in reaching out are the parishes that demand high standards of themselves. And this is part of it. A parish where faith is 'merely believed in' – or largely private, or mainly passive, or deadened, or tangential to life – is hardly going to attract. Parish is meant to be a place of high expectations when it comes to faith. It is a community that challenges itself with the demands of discipleship, always aspiring to a deeper faith.

HEART, HEAD, HANDS

To describe Christian faith in its full reach, I want to explore the image of 'heart and head and hands'. A fully rounded Christian faith includes faith in the heart, faith in the head and faith in the hands. (Chapter nine will add a further dimension to this, in talking of an evangelising faith.)

The story of Martha and Mary (Luke 10) is a good example of these types of faith. Martha's faith is expressed in what she does, in her hands. Mary's faith, sitting and conversing with Jesus, is more of the heart and head. The two women are like external and internal aspects of faith. And it is probably true that, for most people, faith tends to be mainly one or other of the three. Some people work out of their heads, others out of their hearts, others out of their hands. That is the main way in which their faith is expressed and the main way it is nourished.

At the Reformation, there was a sharp contrast between faith and works, heart and hands. But it was never meant to be either/or. Another contrast was between head and heart. Catholic discourse often spoke of faith as the mind's assent to truths revealed by God. Protestant discourse spoke of faith as the heart's surrender to God's action. Again, it was never meant to be either/or.

Head, hands, heart are mutually supportive aspects of a fully rounded faith. Faith in the hands incarnates faith in the heart and head. Faith in the heart deepens faith in the head and hands. Faith in the head enriches faith in the heart and hands. If any of the three stands alone, or if any of the three is neglected, faith is not fully rounded, not whole.

THE HEART

First we will consider faith in the heart. Faith is more than 'what' we believe, more than our beliefs. Christian faith is not so much 'what' as *who*. It is a relationship with God, with Christ. It is 'heart to heart'. Faith in the heart includes elements of trust, of prayer and of belonging.

Trust

Faith in the heart begins with God. In the Bible, the people's experience of God was of One who was faithful, a God of utter faithfulness. God 'keeps faith forever' (Psalm 146:6). God says, 'I will betroth you to me for ever' (Hosea 2:19, NIV). Again, 'if we are faithless, he remains faithful – for he cannot deny himself' (2 Timothy 2:13). Faithfulness is what God is.

God's faithfulness gives our faith the character of trust. God is frequently portrayed with images such as 'rock' or 'fortress'. 'Trust in the Lord forever, for in the Lord God you have an everlasting rock' (Isaiah 26:4). Faith means heartfelt trust in this God who is reliable, solid, sure. It is like a little child resting in its mother's arms (Psalm 131:2).

Trust is also a trust in the process. The letter to the Hebrews quotes Abraham as a model of faith. 'By faith Abraham obeyed when he was called … and he set out, not knowing where he was going' (11:8). God is a God of promise, leading us into God's future. Faith as heartfelt trust means confidently allowing ourselves to be led by God's promise.

It is not all plain sailing. Trust is tested; by misfortune, by illness, by injustice, by death. One major test for God's people was the apparent unfairness of life, how the innocent suffer while wicked people prosper. God seems unmoved, and people are oppressed by God's silence. This makes faith-as-trust real. It is not naïve – it has been through the mill.

For Christians, Jesus is the true face of God, God's faithfulness incarnate. Faith is a relationship with him. Jesus is the good shepherd, the one who can be totally trusted (John 10:11). Again and again in the gospels, we come upon this relationship of trust. Again and again Jesus says to people he heals, 'your faith has made you well' (Matthew 9:22). In faith they are responding to his invitation to trust: 'come to me … and I will give you rest' (Matthew 11:28).

Prayer

Relationships require attention; they cannot be taken for granted. Partners in a relationship take time out to be together, away from tasks and duties, time for themselves. Prayer is when we take time simply to be with Jesus. As in any relationship, there are different ways to be together, different ways to spend the time, heart to heart. They include:

❖ *Silence*. Prayer need have no words. Even if only for a brief 'mindfulness moment', we cease from activity, simply to be present to one another.

❖ *Adoration*. Adoration is how we relate as creatures to our loving creator. We adore and praise the One who brought us into being and invites us to divine Communion.

❖ *Thanks*. We learn to give thanks for God's faithful presence, whether things are good or bad, happy or sad. As we do, we grow into thankful people.

❖ *Listening*. This could be called 'the 7 p.m. prayer'. We 'replay the tape' of the day. We become aware of where we missed God. We learn to live more attentively.

❖ *Lamentation*. As in the Psalms, this may be the most recurrent prayer to God. We plead for help or deliverance. Or we just pour out our troubles to our loving Lord.

- ❖ *Contrition.* This is the prayer of open-heartedness. We allow divine compassion touch all the dark and vulnerable places in our hearts, our fears and our failures.
- ❖ *Other-Centred.* We leave aside our own concerns and become more aware of others around us and their situation. We bring them into our prayer.

These are some ways of praying, just some of the ways of being together with Jesus, heart to heart. Faith and trust are nourished through this heartfelt presence.

Belonging

Faith in the heart is not just about 'me'. Faith in the heart is also *us*. The Acts of the Apostles says that 'the whole group of those who believed were of one heart' (4:32). So, alongside faith in the heart being a feeling of trust, it is also a feeling of belonging. Faith in the heart is vertical (the Lord) and it is horizontal (one another). The two are meant to go together because, while faith is very personal, it is not private. Faith is a together thing.

We have all had the feeling that comes with entering a room and not being noticed at all. If that kind of thing kept happening it would break your heart. You would lose heart. Likewise faith in the heart; faith can lose heart without togetherness. This may be especially so today when, more than ever, Christians will need the support of one another to keep faith alive in their hearts.

Faith-as-belonging is central to the Eucharist. This is where the prayer of our heart becomes communal prayer. The Eucharist itself has its origins in the table-fellowship of Jesus with outsiders, with people who were out in the cold. The experience of welcome and belonging lifted their hearts and restored hope where there had been none. This human encounter was, in turn, a divine experience; the experience of God's welcoming heart. Our Eucharist is meant to be like this.

One key moment in the Eucharist, often unnoticed, is when the priest says, 'Lift up your hearts.' This is our table-fellowship. It is meant to communicate welcome and belonging. In the human feeling of belonging, of being 'of one heart', we are meant to feel divine welcome. It is meant to be 'uplifting', to give us new heart. Belonging encourages and supports faith in the heart.

THE HEAD

Faith in the head sounds like simply a matter of what we believe in. It sounds like beliefs, doctrines, knowledge. That is true, but in a different way than it sounds. 'Knowing' can mean the content of what we believe; it can mean catechism, theology, explanations, theories. But that is secondary knowledge. It is secondary to a knowing that is more important. That is the knowledge of love.

The 14th Century spiritual classic, *The Cloud of Unknowing*, says that God 'cannot be comprehended by our intellect', but that it is 'only to our intellect is he incomprehensible: not to our love'(chapter four). In loving God, a person 'knows' God in a way that is impossible otherwise. Thus faith in the heart leads to faith in the head. It leads to the knowing that is born of love.

Paul talks of this knowledge. 'I regard everything as loss because of the surpassing value of knowing Christ Jesus my Lord ... I want to know Christ and the power of his resurrection' (Philippians 3:8, 10). It is not book knowledge. It is relationship knowledge, personal knowledge. It is like the way one person in a relationship knows the other. It is the knowing that comes from relating to one another.

Personal Knowing

For this kind of knowledge, this faith in the head, we need to go behind the beliefs and the doctrines. We need to connect with the experience from which the beliefs and doctrines originated.

EXPERIENCE

CONFESSION

DOCTRINE

Recall what was said earlier about how Trinitarian faith evolved among the first Christians. What came first was the experience, their encounter with Jesus in his life, death and resurrection. Then came their confession of faith, the belief in Jesus as Lord. With this the Trinitarian language emerged, language which articulated the meaning of the experience for them. Much later came the doctrine, after centuries-long reflection and debate on just what exactly was (and was not) meant by talking of God as Trinity and of Jesus as both human and divine.

What can happen after that third stage is that the doctrines can lose their moorings. They can be truncated from the original experience. If that happens they become dry formulae. People assent that Jesus is 'fully human fully divine'. People assent to 'one divine person, three divine natures'. But do they know as the disciples knew? The disciples did not have the doctrines, but they had the experience and the confession of faith it generated. Could it be that we sometimes have the doctrines, but without the originating experience?

Faith in the head is not just about knowing the doctrines, having the doctrinal knowledge. It is about sharing the same experience as the first disciples and coming to the same confession of faith. If we had as much as they had, we would have so much more than if we had only the doctrines. Faith in the head is personal knowing.

Amazement

A good word for this kind of knowing, this faith in the head, is amazement. Significantly, this is one of the first resurrection words. Peter went from the tomb 'amazed at what had happened' (Luke 24:12). This kind of knowing is more about realising something of great consequence. It is more like a revelation. It is knowledge filled with amazement at what God is doing.

The Christian is somebody who has 'heard' the Good News of the Gospel in this way. He or she has heard it in a way that begins to grasp its import or significance – what it is saying about Jesus; what it is saying about God; what it is telling us about ourselves, our world, our destiny. To hear in this way is to be amazed; and also, perhaps, to share both the 'fear and great joy' of the original disciples (Matthew 28:8).

Faith in the head means grasping the 'bigger picture' in a spirit of amazement. Without this spirit, it may be no more than book knowledge or notional assent. But this also means that faith in the head has to be repeatedly re-amazed. We saw how faith in the heart is nourished by prayer and by belonging. Faith in the head is nourished and re-amazed particularly by reading the Scriptures, especially the Gospels and the New Testament.

Catholics have a poor tradition of reading the Bible. Previous generations regarded it almost as a Protestant book! We are still feeling the effects, in the number of people who are unfamiliar with the Bible and unused to reading it. Still, it is changing; more people are reading Scripture, particularly in the meditative way of *lectio divina*. More and more Catholics are discovering what a relationship with Scripture can mean for their faith.

Here again the Eucharist is central. Faith in the heart is strengthened by the feeling of belonging when we gather together. Faith in the head is meant to be strengthened by the Liturgy of the Word. But people's lack of familiarity with the Bible makes this a challenge. There is much to be done, both within and beyond the Eucharist, so that 'the breaking of the Word' would be an experience of being re-amazed.

Faith in the head is also nourished by reading and studying theology. This might be what first comes to mind when thinking about the head. Theology can sound bookish, academic, detached from real life; and often it deserves that reputation. Yet people who have read or studied theology have found it deeply rewarding. It has proved to be more than an expansion of knowledge. Theology has been described as 'faith seeking understanding'. The understanding it brings nourishes faith in the head and renews our amazement.

THE HANDS

Jesus' command to 'do this' was, as we saw, in two parts. He commanded the breaking of bread and he commanded the washing of feet. The washing of feet symbolises his teaching that we minister to one another. This is faith in the hands.

Sometimes we talk as if faith were one thing and putting it into practice (the hands) another. It is as if there could be two people with faith; one of whom puts it into practice, the other who does not. The Bible, though, sees it differently. The letter of James says that faith without works is 'dead'. The actual 'works' he has in mind involve helping another who lacks food or clothing. 'Show me your faith apart from your works, and I by my works will show you my faith.' Works are what gives faith life, just like the spirit and the body (2:14–26).

There are strong echoes here with a striking passage in the prophet Jeremiah. He is contrasting people who treat others unjustly with those who 'do justice' by attending to the poor and needy. About the latter, he continues, 'Is not this to know me? says the Lord' (22:16). 'To *know* me' comes as a surprise. Surely this is about behaviour, not knowledge? But, as Jeremiah sees it, knowing is action. In the end we know God with our hands. Faith is something we do.

According to Matthew, this is how Jesus sees things. 'Not everyone who says to me, "Lord, Lord", will enter the Kingdom of Heaven, but only the one who does the will of my Father' (7:21). The story of the sheep and the goats (25:31–46) is the most familiar way he expresses it. 'Just as you did it to one of the least of these' – people who are hungry, thirsty, strangers, naked, sick, imprisoned – 'you did it to me.'

The people Jesus alludes to recall the main themes of our 'Gospel picture' from the last chapter. He talks of caring for people who are hungry, thirsty, naked, sick. He talks of welcoming strangers and visiting prisoners. Welcome and care are central to earthing the Gospel in the faith community. This means that faith in the hands is about being an active member of a ministering community, practising welcome and care.

Sending

The well-known painting of the Last Supper – by the German artist Sieger Koder – is dominated by Jesus bent down washing Peter's feet. In the background are the plate of bread and the cup of wine. I wonder if he intended to make a point about the relative prominence of the two, our ministering to one another and our breaking of bread. The Old Testament prophets named the hypocrisy of ritual without the practice of justice and compassion. Maybe faith in the hands needs to be brought to the fore, to centre stage, because it can be forgotten 'behind' the ritual.

This is not to demote the Eucharist. Rather it is to say that, while Eucharist is central, it is only fully celebrated when it is lived. Indeed, just as faith in the heart and in the head are nourished when we gather, so too faith in the hands. Our Eucharist is meant to strengthen this dimension of faith too. It is meant to inspire us in 'doing' our faith.

This is implicit in the Latin word for Mass, '*missa*'. It has the meaning of 'sent'. Mass is about being sent. Its conclusion is not an ending but a sending. The whole point of the gathering is frustrated if it is not empowering, supportive and encouraging of those present for mission. Faith in the heart is nourished by belonging. Faith in the head is enriched by the Word. But it is all in order that they may transfer to faith in the hands.

In the novel *The Secret Scripture*, one of the characters is a priest, Father Gaunt. Not an attractive person, he is described as having 'no antennae at all for grief'. The description continues with an image that gives eloquent expression to faith in the hands. 'He was like a singer who knows the words and can sing, but cannot sing the song as conceived in the heart of the composer. Mostly he was dry.'[16]

I see the composer as Jesus. The song is the life he lived, his way with people, his vision and imagination, his prayer and compassion, his welcome and care. Faith in the hands comes when Christians make this their own. It is when their hearts are filled with what filled Jesus' heart. Then they are captivated. Then they are amazed. Then their lives are very different from lip service, or a merely 'believed-in' faith. Their lives then sing the song as it was conceived in the heart of Jesus.

In one sense this is a huge challenge, to bring faith out of the church and into life, to go beyond a faith of mere ritual. But in another sense it is already going on, though often unacknow-ledged. Many Christians live lives that are centred on others. Most of it is un-trumpeted; family life, caring for another, a community involvement, a social concern. It is not that it is not going on. But often it is not linked with faith. The connection is not made.

We used to talk of a 'practising Catholic' as somebody who goes to Mass. It is a way of thinking that drives a wedge between faith and action. It reduces faith to ritual. It does not appreciate that there are people whose faith is in mainly in their hands, who may not even go to Mass very often. They too are 'practising'.

EVERY MEMBER MINISTRY

Faith in the heart and head; this is the members of the faith community 'reaching in', in a deeper relationship to Jesus, in a deeper relationship to one another, in a deeper amazement at the Good News of the Gospel. Faith in the hands; this is the members of the faith community 'reaching out', singing the song of welcome, care and compassion as conceived in the heart of Jesus. When this is happening, the parish enters into its calling, its mission of earthing the Good News of the Gospel in this particular time and place.

What we are talking about is what is called 'every member ministry'. The idea comes from Paul's imagery of the church as like a human body, each member uniquely involved (1 Corinthians 12). It is a highly participative way of seeing parish. And it comes out of our consideration of faith. Faith community is everybody. It is everybody living their faith; in the heart, in the head, in the hands.

CHAPTER EIGHT
Who's Who in the Parish

This chapter is about the people in the parish. Vatican II saw the people in the church in a new way. It saw priests in a new way. It saw the relationship of priests and people, their respective roles, their modes of involvement, in a new way. Because of Vatican II, we all have to see ourselves in a new way as members of the faith community.

HOW WE SEE OURSELVES
It will be helpful to take a look back over history in order to appreciate just how big a revolution is involved. Even now, people are still struggling to take on board the new way of seeing ourselves. The reason has to do with how deeply rooted we were in a different way of seeing ourselves.

Participation
In the New Testament, Christianity is a very participative, Spirit-inspired movement. Each person is graced, inspired, energised by the Spirit. Paul lists different gifts, different ways in which the Spirit is manifested in people (1 Corinthians 12; Romans 12). 'Ministry', or service, is one of the words he uses for this. What

each one brings is at the service of all, building up the body. It is a ministering community – 'every member ministry'.

As yet there are no 'priests' or 'laity'. The word priest is used in only two senses in the New Testament. The letter to the Hebrews speaks of Christ as the one high priest, whose death and resurrection have done away with the old (Jewish) priesthood. And in the first letter of Peter, the word refers to everybody, to all Christians together being a 'holy priesthood'.

Of course there are leaders in the community, most notably the apostles. The pattern that gradually emerges is that of a leadership figure accompanied by a kind of council. The leader is called *episkopos*, meaning an overseer, while the council is made up of *presbyteroi*, meaning elders. The *episkopos*, as leader, presides at the Eucharist. The words do not yet have the sense of our 'bishop' and 'priest'.

Clericalisation

As Christianity expanded, it was no longer possible for the *episkopos* to preside at every Eucharist. The solution was for the *presbyteroi* to go to the outlying countryside. Gradually, they became the usual leaders of the Eucharist. They came to be seen as 'priests', that is, in a cultic role. Meanwhile the church came to see itself in terms of 'clergy' and 'laity'. Clergy were now a separate 'order', above everybody else, part of a 'hierarchy' (from the Greek word for priest).

All of this made for a very significant shift of mindset. The focal figure now was not so much a community leader as a priest. The community itself became less and less the participative community of New Testament times. The original 'ministry' was being swallowed up into the ministry of the clergy. They now ministered to the 'laity'. Ministry had become what the clergy did.

By medieval times, Ordination came to be defined as conferring a 'power'. The power in question was the power to change the bread and wine into the body and blood of Christ. Crucially, the reference to community was lost. Leadership – *episkopos* – is clearly a relationship to a community. But here, priesthood stands alone. It was now understood in a way that was independent of any community.

This lies behind the extraordinary elevation of the priesthood in later centuries. Because of his sacred 'power', the priest was in a category apart. He was a figure of mystique; his was an exalted status. Older priests will recall their being told in the seminary that the priest was 'a man apart'. He was taken out of the world. Close relationships were discouraged.

Laity

More recently, the church came to define a role for lay people called the 'lay apostolate'. It had the sense of lay people being the presence of the hierarchy in places where the hierarchy could not go; the secular world, the workplace and so on. It was essentially a matter of helping the clergy with *their* ministry.

By the middle of the 20th Century, the church had become a highly centralised and tightly controlled clerical institution. 'church' meant hierarchy. 'Lay' meant passive, deferential, docile, conforming. Notwithstanding the 'lay apostolate', the people remained secondary, like outsiders looking in. A papal document from the early 20th Century put it starkly;

> The church is essentially an *unequal* society … comprising two categories of persons … the hierarchy and the multitude of the faithful … the one duty of the multitude is to allow themselves to be led, and, like a docile flock, to follow the Pastors.[17]

Revolution

There is a book about the Beatles called *Revolution in the Head*. The title refers to what was going on in the 1960s, but it also captures the spirit of what was going on at the Vatican Council. With the historical background in mind, we can see just how great a revolution it was. The church was coming to see itself in a new way.

A small, but very telling illustration of this change comes from one of the main documents of the Council – that about the church itself. The first draft was compiled by the Vatican 'civil service'. It was very traditional, very clerical. Its chapters were about: the nature of the church militant; membership of the church; the hierarchy; religious orders; the laity; the magisterium; authority and obedience; Church and State; evangelisation; ecumenism.

The assembled bishops were unhappy with this, and their work led to further drafting and redrafting. This led to the final document, which had the following sequence of chapters: the mystery of the church; the people of God; the church is hierarchical; the laity; the universal call to holiness; religious; the pilgrim church; Our Lady.

Something has happened here. There has been a revolution in the head. Mystery now comes first. This takes the focus off church and situates church as part of a bigger picture, at the service of God's reign. 'People of God' now precedes any talk of hierarchy, clergy and laity. Holiness, associated with religious life in previous drafts, is now the call of all Christians.

The church now sees itself as a people, a community, and then, secondary to this, as hierarchically structured. This makes for a corresponding shift of focus from the sacrament of Ordination to the sacrament of Baptism. Baptism is now central. We are moving from a clerical institution to a people's church.

It is a momentous shift in mindset. Even a half-century later, it is still only unfolding. It is still being resisted. But that should be no surprise; given the preceding history, change will be slow, gradual.

We will unpack the new self-understanding further by exploring what it means to be a 'layperson' and a 'priest' in the parish.

WHAT IS A LAYPERSON?

The focus here is on the place of the baptised within the community; their role and their relationship to other roles. The word 'laity' defines that place and role in a particular way. But the word carries with it the baggage of a way of thinking that is being left behind. There has been a revolution in how we think about what it is to be a baptised member of the church. It is now highly participative. The language needs to catch up.

There is something unsatisfactory about a word that defines people in terms of what they are *not*. Lay means 'not clergy'. Indeed, when people try to define the word 'lay', they find it hard to do so without using the word 'not'. In one group, people were asked what the word 'lay' suggested to them. One person said that it brought to mind the spare tyre in the car – useful to be able to call on, not much more than that.

The term is unsatisfactory in more ways still. Other institutions besides the church have their version of clergy and laity – medicine and law, for example. Certainly in the past, the professionals had a clergy-like status, even mystique. And those who sought their services were 'lay' people. So, a priest would be a lay person when it comes to medicine. Lay here means unqualified, ignorant, without a voice. The word carries those same associations in the church.

We have pointed out the need for a strong word to describe someone who has been baptised into the church. Baptism does not make somebody into a layperson! Equally, people who are ordained cease to be laypersons. But what is it that they remain after being ordained? There is the word 'Christian'; there is the word 'disciple'. We need a word that undercuts the language and mindset of clergy and lay.

Baptism

The starting point and the focus is *Baptism*. When church is a people's church (the people of God), Baptism is fundamental. In the clerical church, the sacrament of Ordination was the focus. Ministry was a function of being ordained. The furthest lay people could go was to help in that ministry. Anything they did in the line of ministry was by way of delegation.

But we cannot 'delegate' to someone that which is already their own. Now there is a different basis. Now the reference point is no longer church. It is Christ. All who are baptised participate in the ministry and mission of Christ – that includes the ordained too. Ministry is not a 'churchy' thing, one that depends on Ordination. It is a *Christian* thing, one that depends on Baptism. This puts us back in touch with the New Testament Christians, with us all having a part to play.

To express this, Vatican II draws on the first letter of Peter where it says, 'come to him … to be a holy priesthood' (2:4–5). It speaks of the 'priesthood' of all the baptised, not just that of the clergy. 'Each in its own way,' it says, 'shares in the one priesthood of Christ.' In a similar vein, the council took up the language of Christ's threefold ministry as 'priest, prophet and king'. Hitherto applied to the ordained only, now it is for all the baptised.[18]

The language here does not quite work, and it has failed to catch on. Coming from such a clericalised past, it jars to speak of lay people as priests, not to mention calling them prophets and kings. And yet it is an attempt at language, an effort to articulate the new mindset. Despite the difficulty, something radical is going on.

Unity

The mindset extends also to the idea of holiness. In the past, there had been a kind of two-tier spirituality in the church. It is reflected, for instance, in the idea that virginity was a higher calling than marriage. It was as if religious vocations were the 'honours course'. But now all Christians share the one call to fullness of Christian life; to holiness.

Then there is the Word, vocation, which was so narrowed down that it came to refer only to priests and religious. Now vocation is universal. Being a Christian *is* the vocation. And church is a community of vocation, which is what the New Testament word for church suggests – *ekklesia*, a 'con-vocation', called together. All Christians are called. And they are called together, called into community, called to be the body of Christ.

In all this, there is such a strong sense of *everybody*. Vatican II says, 'There is no such thing as a member who does not have a share in the mission of the whole body.'[19] This goes far beyond a few volunteers 'getting involved' or 'helping out'. It is every member ministry. It is not about volunteers. It is about vocation; and that means everybody.

WHAT IS A PRIEST?

All the parts are interlinked. Rethinking laity means rethinking clergy too. If it does not, then the old mentality will not be budged. We may talk of lay people being gifted with the Spirit and sharing in the church's mission. But it will still be seen, if priesthood is not re-envisaged, as merely helping in the ministry of the clergy.

To understand this rethinking of priesthood, recall Christ's ministry as 'priest, prophet and king'. When it is applied to the ordained, it makes for a threefold role. 'Priest' refers to the sacramental role, especially the Eucharist. 'Prophet' refers to preaching the Word. 'King' refers to leadership and pastoral care ('Pastor' might be better). The new way of seeing church leads to redistributing the weight given to each of these.

This is immediately evident in the language chosen. When the council talks about the priest it generally uses the term 'presbyter' rather than the word 'priest'. Presbyter, already used in the New Testament, would have no real resonance for Catholics now. But 'priest' definitely associates the ordained with his sacramental role, rather than with proclaiming or leading. The council's choice of 'presbyter' invites us to think. It invites the other roles to come more prominently into the picture.

I recall a gathering of priests where I asked what model of priesthood was communicated to them in the seminary. One priest said that he was told his role was to proclaim the Gospel. An older priest remarked, 'Well, you're a Vatican II baby!' When I was training, he said, our role was to administer the sacraments. Here we glimpse the council's new emphasis on the 'prophetic' role, where previously it was all about the sacramental or 'priest' role.

Leadership

It is clear that ways of thinking about the role of 'priest' have changed. But the part that is of interest here is about the leadership role of the priest. A new appreciation of this role is also clear in the documents. For instance; priests 'must discover with faith, recognise with joy, and foster diligently the many and varied charismatic gifts of the laity'.[20] Leadership here is not about authority or power. It is about enabling and empowering. Its aim is to build a ministering community, a community of every member ministry.

This insight comes from making Baptism central. Previously, with ministry tied to Ordination, the role of the laity was defined in terms of that of the clergy, as helping in the ministry of the clergy. But now ministry is tied to Baptism. The role of the clergy is defined in terms of that of all the baptised. In this way, the new sense of the vocation and ministry of all brings out a new sense of the ministry of the priest.

Another story illustrates this. A priest who had spent some years working in the church in Latin America was asked what difference he observed between the church there and the church at home. He answered succinctly. 'In Chile the priest helps the people; in Ireland the people help the priest.' These are the two ways of seeing 'who's who' in the parish. It is the difference between a clerical church and a people's church.

A significant statement on the priest's leadership role can be found in the Catechism. The passage is explaining what the church calls the 'essential difference' between the priesthood of the faithful and that of the ordained;

> While the common priesthood of the faithful is exercised by the unfolding of baptismal grace – a life of faith, hope and charity, a life according to the Spirit – the ministerial priesthood is at the service of the common priesthood. It is directed at the unfolding of the baptismal grace of all Christians.[21]

So the ordained person is priest *and* prophet *and* leader. All three matter. But today it is arguably the third that deserves attention. Tomorrow's church depends on a strong, widespread sense of baptismal calling, on every member ministry. This is still only emerging, still finding its place. Its emergence depends crucially on priests entering into and assuming their leadership role of facilitating the ministry of all.

Eucharistic

This understanding of leadership is rooted in the priest's Eucharistic role. In the past, the priest 'said Mass' and everybody looked on. Now the priest 'presides' and all are co-celebrants. All play their part, led by the priest. Many also assume specific roles or ministries. The priest is no longer the sole sacral figure he was. He is now more the focal point, the one who brings a unity to the whole participation.

This is a symbol for the life of the faith community. In daily life, as in the Eucharist, all are called to an active, participatory faith. And the priest holds it together. It is like an orchestra and conductor. The conductor plays no instrument, but brings all the instruments into play. The conductor works for the harmony that is produced when all are playing their part. Leadership is at the service of every member ministry.

COLLABORATIVE MINISTRY

The term 'collaborative ministry' came to prominence in the 1980s. It reflects the church's new way of seeing 'who's who'. At first it was about collaboration between clergy and laity in a sharing of ministry, where previously there was only the ministry of the priest. Collaborative ministry then became more and more visible in the flowering of a rich variety of different 'ministries' in the parish. Today 'partnership' may be a more attractive word than collaboration.

But collaborative ministry is not just about a few volunteers who work alongside the priest. It is about everybody. In this sense it is only a transitional term and should become redundant. The time will come when the word 'ministry' will simply be understood to mean collaborative ministry, every member ministry.

The underlying idea is that church *is* a participation. Paul says, 'The bread that we break, is it not a sharing in the body of Christ?' (1 Corinthians 10:16). 'Sharing' here translates *koinonia*. It is a communion in the sense of a participation. Church is meant to be focused on the full and active participation of all the people. Collaborative ministry is about a participative faith community.

A Whole Way of Being Church

The point is reinforced if we think about the different forms that partnership can take – if we make a list of 'who' is collaborating with 'whom'. Most obviously it is priests and people. Again, it is school, home and parish working together on First Communion and Confirmation. With less priests, it is neighbouring parishes, and parish areas, coming together. It is parishes here at home twinning with parishes in the developing world. It is religious congregations working together. It is ecumenism, developing bonds between Christian churches.

Less obviously perhaps, collaboration is also between different groups in the parish, which often work in separate, unrelated compartments. It is between parish groups and community groups, building on what they have in common. It is between priests themselves, so often 'lone rangers' before. It is between different agencies within a diocese. It is between dioceses themselves.

Other examples of collaborative ministry are perhaps less obvious still. It is between men and women, still such a challenge for the church. It is between old and young. It is between family members. It is between rich and poor, the gap between them often as great in the church as elsewhere. It is between Christianity and other faiths, especially in Ireland's new multicultural context. It is between the universal church (Rome) and the local churches, in the spirit of 'collegiality' that Vatican II aspired to.

The list could go on. But what is listed is enough to show that the spirit of partnership and participation applies at all levels and involves everybody. It overflows into relationships with others outside of church. It is clearly more than just some new way of doing things. It amounts to a whole way of being church.

A Spirituality
Collaborative ministry goes deeper still. It touches on how we see God. It is an expression of our faith, of what we understand about God. As John Paul II described it, it is a *spirituality*, a spirituality of communion.[22] It reaches deep into what we believe and that reaches into God.

This spirituality has its roots in the New Testament. Jesus' way was to work with others. He chose to work with the twelve apostles. He chose to work with the seventy he sent out in pairs. The same spirit is found in Paul. He begins his letters by introducing his 'co-workers'. He encourages richer communities to support needier ones. He gives us the image of the body of Christ, every member indispensable, enriching and building the whole body.

But the reason collaborative ministry has these roots in Scripture is that it reaches into God. It is an aspect of the God of Jesus Christ. Think of the great Christian themes – the Trinity, Creation, Incarnation, Pentecost, Grace – and see how each of them reflects a God of partnership and participation;

- ❖ *Creation* is when God invites humanity to be co-creators in the unfolding story of the universe, with all the risk that entails.
- ❖ *Incarnation*, the unity of humanity and divinity, is reflected in Mary's 'yes' to God's Spirit working in her, with her and through her.
- ❖ *Trinity* tells us that God is not an 'old man in the sky', but a communion of life and love, both unity and diversity.
- ❖ *Pentecost* is where Jesus entrusts his disciples with continuing his mission by the power of the Spirit.
- ❖ *Grace and freedom*, a major theme in theology, is about the balance between what God is doing in our lives and what we do ourselves.

The message is strong and clear. God's way is the way of partnership. The deepest meaning of collaborative ministry is not our working with one another, but our collaboration with God. And because God's way is that of collaboration, the church and the parish have no choice, other than to be as God is.

I referred to Paul's co-workers. The Greek word is *sunergoi*, and it is suggestive in a way that the Latin *collaboratio* is not. Collaboration means simply 'working with', but synergy has the added sense of something greater that is present when we work together. God's Spirit is released when the way we are as church, as parish, is the way of participation and partnership. Something greater than ourselves is at work.

VOCATIONS CRISIS?

The new 'who's who' in today's church gives us a different perspective on what we call the 'vocations crisis'. This phrase is used in reference to both priests and religious, but usually it is about priests. The most evident crisis is that the priests we have are ageing and growing fewer – there are so few younger priests as the seminaries are empty.

But the key crisis is elsewhere. It is where a large number of baptised people are still in a passive, provided-for mode – still 'laity' in that sense. It is where many baptised people are not in touch with their own Baptism, their faith marginal to their lives, perhaps only a 'believed-in' faith. If all that is true, and if Baptism is the fundamental vocation, then it seems clear that this is the main issue. The challenge revolves around Baptism, not Ordination. It is about every member ministry.

CHAPTER NINE
An Evangelising Parish

This chapter is a bridge between the more reflective sections so far and the more practical sections that follow. It gathers what has been discussed so far, in the idea of tomorrow's parish being an 'evangelising' parish. The five chapters of the next section go into detail about how the evangelising parish expresses itself.

WHAT IS EVANGELISATION?

We need to start with the word itself, because evangelisation means different things to different people. It can bring to mind the evangelist preaching repentance; the televangelist persuading you to accept Jesus Christ as your personal Lord and Saviour; Mormons or Jehovah's Witnesses knocking on the door. It can be associated with being on an emotional high, or exploiting fears and vulnerabilities, or even manipulation.

Then there is the related word 'mission'. While central to our discussion, it has off-putting connotations too. While missionaries have done enormous good, we now see also the darker side. We see the condescension; we the enlightened, they the 'pagans'. We see the arrogance; we possessing the truth, suppressing the indigenous faith, no sense that God might already be there before us.

Having cleared the way a little, we can concentrate on the positive meaning of the word. Evangelisation comes from the Greek word *ev*, meaning 'well', and *angel*, meaning message. Join these together and we have 'good message'; or it could also mean good news, message of good news, messenger announcing good news. In everyday life it could have meant, for example, a messenger bringing back news of victory in battle.

The New Testament transposes this into a religious context. There evangelisation means announcing the Good News of what God is doing in Jesus Christ. Originally 'Gospel' – *evangelion* – was simply the Good News itself (as with the old English word godspell or good message). It was a while before Christians came to talk of the gospels as literature, and of the authors as 'evangelists'.

So, evangelisation is a very positive word. Its mood is joy. It is about something really worth sharing and really worth finding out about. A good definition might be that evangelisation is about introducing people to Jesus Christ. It happens when somebody comes to encounter him, when they begin to glimpse who he is and start to appreciate the Good News he represents.

The word 'introducing' has the feeling of something gracious. To 'introduce' people to Jesus Christ is something done graciously. It is not proselytising or manipulating or corralling them into the faith. It is more the spirit of offering something. It is filled with respect for people and where they are in their lives. And – a key point in all that follows – words are only part of how it is done. We 'speak' through how we act towards others. What people 'hear' is what we do and how we relate to them.

EVERYTHING

Evangelisation is very much what we have been talking about, without actually using the word. We have made church and parish part of the bigger picture of God's mission to the world in Christ. We have seen church and parish as partners in the divine mission. That is evangelisation. We have spoken of the parish's mission to Earth the Gospel, the Good News. That is evangelisation.

This leads us to see that evangelisation is the very identity of church and parish. It is not simply one of the things that the church does. It is not simply one activity among many. And, especially today, it is not an emergency response to a crisis. Rather, it is *everything*. It is the essence of what church and parish are about. In a sense, it is the *only* thing the church does. Thus Paul VI wrote;

> The task of evangelising all people constitutes the essential mission of the church ... her deepest identity. She exists in order to evangelise ... is linked to evangelisation in her most intimate being.[23]

EVERYBODY

Evangelising is the activity of everybody. Anyone born into the faith community in Baptism is born into this. Pope Francis puts it eloquently. Baptism makes us all 'missionary disciples'. The fact that we have 'encountered the love of God in Christ Jesus' itself makes each of us a missionary;

> All the baptised, whatever their position in the church or their level of instruction in the faith, are agents of evangelisation, and it would be insufficient to envisage a plan of

evangelisation to be carried out by professionals while the rest of the faithful would simply be passive recipients ... Every Christian is challenged.[24]

This is a further dimension of faith, as we discussed in chapter seven. Being a disciple means aspiring to an ever richer faith in the heart, in the head, in the hands. But an essential dimension is that this faith is always an outgoing faith. This is every member ministry. It is expressed especially through 'faith in the hands'.

To talk about evangelising in this way may be new. And yet, if evangelising is not a part of how the faith community and all its individual members see themselves, then we are not fully in touch with our Christian selves. We may be locked into routine, into comfort and complacency. Instead, we need to be making this central to our Christian lives.

Being Evangelised

The idea of introducing people to the Good News could sound as if there are two categories, those who evangelise and those who are evangelised. It could give the impression that, as more people are evangelised, there are then less people to be evangelised. And that is misleading.

A key part of it is that everybody is called to evangelise *and* everybody is called to be evangelised. The call to be evangelised continues for everybody. Francis talks about 'the first proclamation', when first we heard the Good News. But it is called first 'not because it exists at the beginning and can then be forgotten ... It is first ... because it is the *principal* proclamation, the one which we must hear again and again in different ways.'[25]

Paul VI said the same. When he uses the word 'church' here, we should each take it as being addressed to ourselves;

> The church is an evangeliser, but she begins by being evangelised herself ... she needs to listen unceasingly to what she must believe ... she has a constant need of being evangelised, if she wishes to retain freshness, vigour and strength in order to proclaim the Gospel ... in order to evangelise the world with credibility.[26]

This 'self-evangelisation' is not something occasional. It is an ongoing process, whether church is strong or weak, whether an individual's faith is strong or weak, at any given time. It is a permanent part of being a Christian and being a faith community. We talk of the sacraments of 'initiation', but in fact Christians are a community of ongoing initiation. The life of the faith community is a process of being initiated ever more deeply into their Baptism identity.

The greatest contribution anyone can make to evangelisation is to lead a profound Christian life. Self-evangelisation is the way to this. We open ourselves to being evangelised, out of a complacent, merely 'believed-in' faith, into an ever richer faith in the heart, in the head, in the hands. We open ourselves to being evangelised, out of a passive, 'provided-for' faith, into an ever stronger participative faith, our every member ministry. A big part of it is opening ourselves to being evangelised by the faith and witness of others around us.

From this depth of 'inreach' we reach out. When we have this depth, we embody the Good News. Then we 'retain freshness, vigour and strength'. Together we present a 'version' of Christianity which is credible and which is attractive. This is what others will listen to.

'NEW EVANGELISATION'

We turn now to the reaching out. Outreach is a relatively recent addition to the vocabulary of the parish. It does not carry the baggage of words like mission and evangelisation. The word is a product of changing times, of the realisation that it will not do for the church to stay absorbed in its own inner life. It captures the need to move out from comfort and complacency, and to re-engage with the larger community.

It is also an attractive word, very much in the same spirit as the phrase of 'introducing' people to Jesus Christ. It has that same mood of offering. It does not want to pressurise or manipulate. It approaches the other graciously and, conscious of its own need to be evangelised, humbly. But it also has a mood of confidence, believing that there is something really worthwhile for the other to know about and experience.

But who is it that we reach out to? Words like mission and evangelisation can sound as though it is non-Christians we are reaching out to, people who have not heard the Gospel. It may of course be the case in some instances. But mostly in Ireland, it is to people who are baptised into the church, but who may not have gone much further than that.

'New evangelisation' is the term now in currency for this outreach to the already baptised. It comes from John Paul II and his attention to this issue. He speaks of the situation

> in countries with ancient Christian roots ... where entire groups of the baptised have lost a living sense of the faith, or even no longer consider themselves members of the church, and live a life far removed from Christ and his Gospel. In this case what is needed is a 'new evangelisation' or a 're-evangelisation'.[27]

It is a novel way of thinking. Hitherto, mission or evangelisation was directed specifically towards people who were not baptised. Now evangelisation is also directed to people *already* baptised. It is addressed to people who no longer engage with church, or perhaps never had an experience of belonging in the faith community, or who no longer profess Christian faith.

LISTENING AND LOVING

There is no clear demarcation here of 'insider' from 'outsider'. It is more like a continuum among all the baptised. Things may be clear at the extreme ends: at one end, those who are strongly engaging with faith and faith community; at the other, those who are decisively disengaged. But a great many of the baptised are somewhere in between – and some of them churchgoers, some of them not!

We talked about people 'out there' in chapter two. We spoke of how much salvation is going on outside of church. While many are lost or searching, many are not. Many who have left the church have found something else. Many are living a spiritual life in a way they have worked out for themselves. Many are travelling spiritual journeys that leave much of what goes on within church lagging behind. But also, while many are living life at a depth apart from church, they are not necessarily averse to a new engagement. In some, there is a spark, perhaps waiting to be rekindled.

To listen to all this is to evangelise and to be evangelised. We reach out, not simply to bring God, but to meet God. We reach out to appreciate and to learn. We hope that, in our respect and our listening, people will 'hear' of a God who respects them and who listens attentively to their life story. Maybe listening will lead to their wanting to be introduced, or re-introduced, to Jesus Christ.

But there are no ulterior motives. We do not worry. We know that God is already there in people's lives, God's Spirit in every heart. We reach out from that disposition; to listen, to dialogue, to learn. There is no hidden agenda, but there is a hope. Our hope is that we can offer an enlightenment about the God who is already there, the enlightenment that comes from the Good News, the Gospel.

Outreach is listening, but mainly it is love. This links immediately with Jesus' own ministry. It is clear from what was said in chapters five and six that Jesus reached out mainly by what he did, with his care and compassion, his welcome and inclusion. He 'spoke' through what he did. But he spoke in words too, the words accompanying the action. So, for example, we have his action of table-fellowship with outcasts on one hand, and his words on the other, words of God's Kingdom being like a banquet to which all are invited.

This is the model for our outreach, action accompanied by words. Our aim – the 'why' we reach out with loving action – is that people will 'hear' the Good News. Our hope is that others will know, through our love, that they are loved by God. Maybe they know that already, maybe they do not. And maybe, if people 'hear' this, it will be the start of an introduction, or re-introduction to Jesus Christ.

This model of reaching out – of evangelisation through actions mainly, but also through words – will be taken up in the four themes of the next section – the themes of caring, of welcoming, of listening and of praying.

An Analogy

Finally, I want to reflect on marketing as an analogy for the activity of the evangelising parish. Some will warm immediately to the analogy. Others will see it as inappropriate. But an analogy is just that; similar in some respects, not all. As such it has something worthwhile to offer.

In marketing language, evangelisation is about selling a product. In this case the product is the Good News of God's love for humanity in Christ. But today the product has been dismissed by many as obsolete. It is discredited through scandals and dysfunctionality within the church. It seems that a new marketing effort is required, to re-package and re-launch the product.

And yet, in the 1960s, at the Vatican Council, the church was engaged in the greatest 're-launch' in its history. More than just a re-packaging, it was a rethinking of the product at a deep level. Today's new marketing effort is about really absorbing that thinking and putting it into practice. It is about expressing ourselves as an evangelising parish.

Of course there are reservations about marketing as an analogy for evangelisation. Marketing is profit-driven; but the only profit sought in evangelisation is the good of the other. The product is free and offered freely. Again, evangelisation cherishes freedom, whereas marketing can bypass freedom and can manipulate. Evangelisation appeals to what is highest in the other person, while marketing often appeals to fears and insecurities.

But evangelisation can have its dark side too. It can be self-centred and self-interested. It can be more concerned with increasing its numbers than the good of the people. It can disrespect freedom. It can look to control people's behaviour. It can seek to colonise people's minds. It can demand mindless obedience.

Already the comparison is helping to illuminate evangelisation at its best and at its worst. But my main interest here is what evangelisation can learn from marketing. I have three lessons in mind. It can learn about re-amazement. It can learn about listening. It can learn about witness.

First, successful marketing has a strong sense of its product. It believes in the product and is enthused about it. It has a clear sense of what is distinctive and inimitable about it. It is focused about what it has to offer. This links with our idea of self-evangelisation.

Those who evangelise need to *know* their product. Evangelisation has often misunderstood its own product; for instance, thinking it is church rather than Gospel, damnation rather than salvation, sin rather than love. Those who evangelise need to be *enthused*. They need to go back to the well, to be re-amazed, so that outreach is coming from a deep place within. They need a clear sense of what the Gospel has to offer in a world that is spiritually rich.

Second, successful marketing has a strong sense of its audience. Just think of the huge sums invested in researching the audience. Whether it be teenagers or young mothers, retired people or farmers, marketing goes to great lengths to get inside their world and to understand their concerns so as to connect the product with their needs and desires. This links with our idea of listening.

Evangelisation has often been one-way traffic, with little or no interest in people's own beliefs and values, needs and concerns. Today those who evangelise need to enter into the situation of the other. Before making 'them' aware of 'us' there is need to make 'us' aware of 'them'. This awareness will be the basis for any connection made, for any relevance the product may be seen to have.

Third, successful marketing is characterised by quality communication. Advertising shows this. The message is graphic. The language is sharp. The effect is striking. The impression is lasting. On TV, the ads can be more interesting than the programme they interrupt! Attraction and captivation are everything. This links to the idea of witness.

Evangelisation is challenged to be persuasive in its communication. Sometimes those who evangelise act as though it is a matter merely of imparting information. But the word is only fully spoken when it is heard. To be heard, it needs to be spoken eloquently, and that means the eloquence of Christian living, of faith in the hands – the attractiveness of witness that can captivate hearts.

SECTION C

Expressing Ourselves

CHAPTER TEN
Caring

The chapters in this section portray the evangelising parish – tomorrow's parish – in action. Through the themes of caring, welcoming, listening and praying, together with the theme of family, we describe how tomorrow's parish expresses itself. They are not the only ways of describing the parish, but they emerge naturally from what has gone before and, indeed, have been prominent already in our discussion.

Each of these themes is a kind of invitation to the parish. Each of them says to the parish; 'think about me'. The idea is that the faith community would allow itself to be led by each of these themes. If it does, it will find itself being led into its own identity, its own future, as an evangelising parish. The five themes are paths to self-realisation.

'WE CARE THAT YOU EXIST'

We begin with caring. The parish is a ministering community. Ministry, though, is not seen as an everyday word. But listen to the story of Jesus' time in the desert, his intense life-defining spiritual struggle. It says how the angels came and 'ministered' to him (Mark 1:13, Knox translation). That brings the word down to Earth. It is precious, yet ordinary. They took care of him. In Irish, the words ministry and care come together in the word *aire*.

We can readily identify with this down-to-earth ministering in our own lives. We can recall occasions of giving ministry and occasions when we received ministry, of caring and being cared for. We have known care in our need, and we have responded to need with our care. We can see how care is the fundamental response of one person to another. It is a short step from this to seeing the caring parish as a place of every member ministry.

There is a phrase that has stayed with me since a discussion some years ago in one parish. The members of the parish council were sharing what the word 'parish' meant to them. One person used this phrase: 'We care that you exist.' It is a powerful way of expressing what the evangelising parish is about, or can be about.

'We care that you exist.' Who might the 'you' be? A family grieving? A parent who has lost their job? A home torn apart by substance abuse? Mostly it is not something so dramatic. Someone who has been housebound for years. Someone else unable to establish relationships. A deep feeling of loneliness. People who cannot forgive themselves. Most suffering is silent, unseen.

All of us suffer. It may be in ways that are less extreme, but it is no less real. It may be that you cannot understand your children – or your parents. It may be that you cannot find peace, or that you feel you have wasted years. It may be that you are carrying a burden, or that you are looking for love. It may be that you are trying too hard, or that you see no way forward.

The evangelising parish wants to say, 'we care that you exist'. The only way to express this is to notice and to *care*. The desire is inspired by the care expressed by Jesus for so many people, in so many different situations of pain or suffering or need. It is inspired by Jesus, in whom we see the face of God; in whom we hear the Good News of God's passionate care for us; in whom we hear the call to be the Good News of God's care today.

How does the faith community, the parish, realise this? How does it make the words 'we care that you exist' a reality? There are two parts to my answer. First, I will reflect on how this is *already* happening in the parish. Second, I will consider the *not yet*, what still needs to happen to make it a reality.

ALREADY

Starting with the already, I want to highlight the significance of affirmation. There is a hugely significant and largely overlooked task involved in affirming the caring that already goes on in the faith community. Here we are asked to do nothing new. Instead we are asked to pay attention to what is *already* going on. There is so much already happening that we may not acknowledge it. Often, people themselves do not recognise it.

By way of illustration, a priest recounted his conversation with a woman in the parish. She said to him, 'Now that I've reared my family, I'd like to do something for the church.' We can see what she meant; perhaps she wanted to give something back. But was there also something that she missed? Maybe she did not see that bringing up her family was her primary way of being involved in the parish.

Most of what I am talking about is ordinary, almost too ordinary to command attention. Most of it happens in families. And here I am thinking of all the different kinds of 'family' today, including lone parents and their children, unmarried partners and their children, couples in a second relationship, same-sex partnerships, childless couples. All are engaged in the same family activities of caring, protecting, nurturing, supporting and healing.

Of all the ways in which people care, the care of parents for children is pre-eminent, in its passion and its other-centred concern. It is about building the family itself into a community of care. It is about building a community where belonging and being loved teach us what it means to be a human being. It is about learning to say 'we' and not just 'me', about learning to be a person for others.

The family is the basic Christian community. It is the basic place where people live the Gospel, where they express faith in the hands. That is part of why family prayer is so important. It helps people to realise that their family relationships, of caring and being cared for, are about becoming more Christian and becoming a little community of disciples.

But caring goes on in all kinds of ways. It is happening all the time in friendships, in the sharing and listening and responsiveness of companions. It is happening in the courtesy and helpfulness and support of neighbours. It is happening when people care for someone who is sick or lonely or depressed, be it family or friend or neighbour.

Many people see their work as an expression of care, most obviously in areas such as healthcare and education. Many devote a lot of time to running sports clubs for the children. Others are involved in St Vincent de Paul, meals on wheels, soup runs. Others give time to groups that support people who are bereaved, or accompany people who are sick or housebound. Others care through counselling. Others again are committed to forms of community development or social justice.

There are an uncountable number of ways in which we care, more than can fit here. It is worth noting that some of this is faith-inspired and some not. Some people see their care as faith in the hands. But others who share similar passions are not coming from a place of faith. Their care is an expression of their humanity. In this sense, it is spiritual. They are living at depth.

Affirmation

My main point here is that the caring parish will place a high priority on affirming this care. There is huge potential for parishes to do a lot more to acknowledge and to affirm the care that goes on within the faith community.

Affirmation does a number of things. For starters, it is always encouraging for people when what they do is noticed. In terms of faith, it helps people see God in what they are doing. It makes a connection between ordinary everyday life and church. It helps people see that religion is not a separate compartment of life. It testifies that religion is about how life is lived and how we care for one another.

Affirmation deepens discipleship. A person's faith can be at a low level of activation. Maybe there is a prayer now and then, an occasional Mass, an intermittent sense of God. Making the connection can change that. People can name the 'ministering' going on in their life. In the process, God is becoming a more living presence for them.

It is as if their Baptism is being 'activated'. They are coming to see the underlying meaning in how they have been living their lives. Through this process they are entering into their own discipleship, their every member ministry. They are coming to see themselves as active members of a ministering parish.

As well as this, affirmation can be the springboard for supporting people in their every member ministry of caring. Think of parents, for whom so much can be done by way of affirmation. That can develop into ways of supporting them in their role as faith-companion or faith-leader for their children, for instance through resources for family prayer. Affirmation creates an awareness of discipleship, which can lead into the building of disciples.

Opportunities for Affirmation

Sunday is an important time for affirmation (though relevant mainly for those who attend). It happens too often that, when people go to Mass, they have to leave their lives at the porch. No connections will be made between what goes on in the church and the concerns of their everyday lives. It will be like entering another world for an hour or so. The homily and the prayers will be about something else. And then it will end and people will return to normal mode.

It can be different. People's lives and concerns can be gathered into the celebration. For example, somebody told a story of a time she was at Mass. The priest was talking about mission, and the mission we each have as Christians. Whatever way his words worked, she began to reflect. 'I have been minding my infirm sister all these years. Yet only today have I come to see this as my mission. I have been living this ministry all the time without knowing it.' This is an example of the kind of connection many more people can be helped to make.

Affirmation can be built into other sacramental occasions also, where many of those present go to church less frequently. In Baptism, First Communion and Confirmation liturgies, there can be a strong message of encouragement and appreciation of the parents in their role of care. The affirmation can make a connection between the care they show and the faith within. The time of a funeral is also a time to acknowledge and give thanks, for caring and being cared for. This too can re-establish a faith connection.

Another way of affirming concerns those who are involved in the parish. All ministries are forms of care, while some parish ministries have care as their specific focus. All ministries can be encouraged and supported by affirmation. The affirmation can also highlight how this ministering is a 'mirror' to all in the faith community, reflecting back to them their own vocation to care.

The parish can also explore ways of affirming people involved in caring that is not parish-based, both those whose care is faith-inspired and those with different inspirations. One possibility might be an event for 'celebrating the voluntary', bringing together a broad spectrum of individuals and groups where care, rather than faith, is the common denominator.

Including groups whose care is not specifically faith-inspired is not to 'corral' them; it is to acknowledge, and to affirm. It is also a way of saying that the faith community is enriched by them, challenged by them, evangelised by them. It could also be a step towards building bridges, forging links, and generating dialogue and collaboration.

To repeat, affirmation of caring that is already present in the community can be a very significant part of the evangelising parish. It encourages and energises. It connects faith and life. It builds discipleship, and every member ministry. It unites all in a common focus – that of a caring faith community.

NOT YET

The caring that goes on, for all its richness, falls short – probably far short – of all the caring that is needed in the community. Thus far we have looked at ordinary, everyday caring. It includes ministries of care in the parish. It includes what believers do outside a parish context. It acknowledges the caring expressed by people outside the faith community. But whatever may be impressive about the list should not hide its incompleteness. There is more to caring. There always will be.

Caring responds to needs. It responds to suffering. But yet, some needs still go unnoticed, and much suffering is unattended to. I used the phrase 'we care that you exist' for the message that the evangelising parish wants to send out. But the words on their own are weak. How can we care for you if we do not even know you exist?

The 17th Century, French philosopher René Descartes went to live in Amsterdam. Amsterdam was then the foremost city in the world, the capital of commerce and international trade. Descartes wrote, 'In this city there is nobody who does not trade in something. Everyone is so preoccupied by his own profit that I could live here for all my life without ever being noticed by anyone.'[28]

After four more centuries of worldwide urbanisation, the same sentiment could be expressed almost anywhere. We live in a world that does not notice. People are absorbed by their own concerns. Self-interest numbs the senses. Many resist this and try, through their care, to penetrate the numbness. And yet, there are many people who live their lives 'without ever being noticed by anyone'.

Awareness

The caring parish is called to a further step beyond affirmation. It is called to *awareness*, called to notice. Affirmation strengthens people's sense of being a community of disciples, called to care for one another as Jesus taught us. It leads naturally to the next step, of identifying needs that are not being addressed, of reaching out further, of creating the care that is 'not yet'.

Sometimes reaching out has a church-centred motive, to make 'them aware of us'. But the next step I am talking about in caring is about making 'us aware of them'. It brings to mind God's words in Exodus: 'I have observed the misery of my people who are in Egypt; I have heard their cry … I know their sufferings' (Exodus 3:7). Our God is aware. Our God notices.

And it recalls the gospels. Jesus notices. He sees how his friends are struggling with the storm on the lake. Just before that, as he looked on the crowd, 'he had compassion for them, because they were like sheep without a shepherd' (Mark 6:34). He is aware. He is God with a human face.

But also, Jesus does not rest content. When his companions tell him that everybody is searching for him, he answers, 'Let us go on to the neighbouring towns, so that I may proclaim the message there also' (Mark 1:38). The caring parish moves on, just as Jesus does. It turns its attention to the 'not yet'. It looks for the not-yet-noticed, the not-yet-cared-for.

The caring parish seeks to become aware, to notice, to see what the Lord sees. And what God is drawn to most is suffering and need. That is the divine compassion. Allowing ourselves to notice means allowing ourselves, like the Lord, to be affected. Being affected is the birth of divine compassion in us.

Creating Awareness
How do we do this? We have to go out to find out, do we not? We have to shift into a different mode. We have to 'move on'; out of the church, away from what we are absorbed with in running our parishes, beyond any complacency or feeling satisfied with our achievements. We have to break out of our own numbness and not noticing. And we have to break through the silence, the unseen-ness of so much need and suffering. The following are some possible ways to create awareness and become affected.

One possibility is to visit. The parish could organise a visitation project, recruit a team to go out in pairs. (Admittedly, gated houses and apartment blocks make it hard to access everybody.) I have in mind a doorstep conversation of no more than a few minutes, 'armed' with an attractive flyer about 'our caring faith community'. The aim is simple: to present the friendly, caring face of the parish in the friendliness of those calling.

For the people being called on, it would be an invitation or opportunity to let the callers know of any need they are aware of that could be responded to. I am thinking of two parishes that carried out such an initiative, both of which discovered an amount of loneliness that they had been unaware of. Or it could be as simple as coming across sick people who would appreciate a regular call or a hospital visit.

Another idea is to set up a network of neighbourhood contact persons. Each person would be the eyes and ears of the caring parish for their own street or locality. They would commit to becoming more aware of their neighbours, and of their needs and struggles. These people would meet occasionally to share their observations. Patterns might emerge and avenues of response might begin to suggest themselves.

A related idea is focus groups. This will be discussed in the chapter on listening. It involves a group of people, possibly with a similar life experience, researching the situation and needs of a particular category of people in the parish (e.g. young people, bereaved people, and so on). Again, coming together to share findings would bring up challenges for caring.

Another approach is through parish communications media; newsletters, websites and Facebook. These would be utilised to project the message of the caring parish – 'we care that you exist'. People could be invited to give feedback on what they see around them, whatever they think is inviting the response of the faith community. People might also be asked to register any interest they themselves might have in being part of a specific response.

Finally, there are possibilities at Sunday Mass. Besides affirming people, the homily and prayers can encourage them to become aware of needs and struggles and suffering around them. Homilies could also include presentations from people with direct experience of different areas of care and need. Again, it is all helping to build every member ministry.

Part of being a parish is to look beyond the parish. So a further dimension is the need and suffering that exist beyond the parish – in the larger society, in the world. Some members of the faith community are already engaged in caring on that front. Special collections at Mass for the poor, or to help with some disaster abroad, are further examples. So is twinning with a parish from the developing world. A caring parish grows in awareness of that bigger world. It encourages members to be part of a caring response.

Out of the different efforts to build awareness, specific needs will surface. This can then be presented back to the faith community; at Mass, in the newsletter, or on the website. There could be a special gathering after Mass every now and then; something practical, very brief (fifteen minutes or so) and really well focused. Mobilising a response is more likely (a) if the background work of affirming the community has been going on, and (b) if what is sought is a specific, manageable, short-term commitment.

THE MAIN VISIBILITY

Earlier I spoke of Sieger Koder's painting of the Last Supper. It places the bread and cup in the background, while Jesus washing Peter's feet takes up the centre and foreground. In both actions Jesus says 'Do this in memory of me'. He tells us to gather for the breaking of bread. He tells us to care for one another as he did.

What occupies the foreground is what is most visible. When others look on and see the faith community, what do they see? What do people see when they see 'church'? What they are meant to see is more than the Mass-going. What they are meant to see is not just a community at prayer, but a community at care. Caring is the main visibility of the evangelising parish. It is how we put ourselves forward. It is how we express ourselves. It is where people see who we are.

More importantly, it is where people see who God is. We speak of God as beyond all seeing, the utterly unknowable One. We also speak (in one of the prayers at Mass) of Jesus as God made visible, so that we are caught up in the love of the God we cannot see. The caring parish is the 'today' of this. In its caring, the faith community makes visible the God beyond all seeing.

CHAPTER ELEVEN
Welcoming

People in parishes may not realise how much their way of thinking about parish is now imbued with the Gospel spirit of welcome. Often in working with parish pastoral groups I have invited people to think about what parish is all about. What above all else does parish have to offer people today? What is at the heart of parish?

It is striking how the same words recur again and again in people's responses. The words that come up most are 'belonging' and 'welcome', then 'inclusive', 'accepting', 'community', and the like. This amounts to a strong, widespread intuition about what parish is and what we want it to be today. People say that what they like and cherish about their parishes is the sense of community, of welcome and belonging. Those who are involved in parishes see parish as inviting people into an experience of welcome and belonging. This, perhaps more than anything, is what parishes aspire to today.

This sense of what parish is all about has been growing stronger. More and more it is reflected in what is actually going on in parishes. In fact, it could be argued that most of the life-giving initiatives developed in recent times revolve around welcome and belonging. Think of family Mass, Baptism teams,

First Communion and Confirmation programmes, visitation teams, welcome packs, funeral ministry, and much more. The common denominator is welcome, and its evangelising power to spread the Good News.

A Gospel Intuition

There is a sense, in this intuition and this consensus, of the Spirit speaking to the church.

It is also a Gospel intuition. In chapter six we spoke of how welcome is at the very heart of Jesus' ministry, illustrated most strikingly in his table hospitality to outcasts and sinners. His welcome is inclusive, all-embracing and boundary-breaking. It reaches out beyond his own, to the Samaritan woman at the well, to the centurion, to the Canaanite woman. Welcome pervades the pages of the Gospel.

In his welcome, Jesus is embodying God's welcoming heart. In the story of the great banquet to which all are invited, and in the story of the prodigal son, he imaginatively symbolises the way in which welcome is the heart of God. He proclaims that the Good News is just this; that God's heart is a welcoming heart, that there is none who is beyond God's embrace. Welcome is the heart of God.

The welcoming parish is very much in touch with its roots in the Gospel. The moral is clear: what is at the heart of God is to be at the heart of the church. Welcome is to be the very heartbeat of the faith community. In this spirit, one parish used the following prayer as a kind of mission statement. 'God's heart is a welcoming heart, reaching out in Jesus to embrace all. Our parish dream is that all would feel welcomed and called to welcome.'

It is important to stress that welcome *is itself* the Gospel. It is not a means to an end. It is not that we are welcoming in order that people will then be open to hearing the Gospel. Welcome is itself the evangelisation, just as care is. People found God in the welcome of Jesus, and it is no different today. In our welcome, people 'hear' the Good News of God's welcoming heart.

Equally, it is important to repeat that we are talking about every member ministry. The idea of the welcoming parish is not that a few individuals or groups carry out welcoming projects on behalf of the parish. That is good as far as it goes, but it does not go far enough. The idea is that all would feel 'called to welcome', just as they feel welcomed themselves. That is what the evangelising parish aspires to.

Finally, we do well to remember the contrast that there is in the Gospel. Not only is welcome central, but unwelcome is never far away. The shepherds welcome, the Magi welcome; but Herod lurks in the background. Jesus speaks of how his own people do not accept him; he tells the story of the tenants plotting to kill the heir. While he welcomes sinners and eats with them, the Pharisees and scribes grumble. The father welcomes his prodigal son; but the older brother thinks differently.

This tension invites us to consider the parish from both points of view. First, we will consider the welcoming that has been going on and that can spread further abroad. Second, we will consider what may be unwelcoming about our parishes and the challenge that poses.

POSSIBILITIES
What follows is a list of possibilities, ideas for becoming a more welcoming parish. Generally, these are possibilities that are already being realised in many places. They include the different life-giving initiatives I referred to at the start of the chapter.

Hospitality
Let us start with the family Mass. It has become the big weekend Mass in a lot of parishes. It revolves around welcome. Imagine the

scene. The parents used to bring their young child to Mass. The child made noise; somebody looked around and scowled ... the message was clear. But here, instead, it is family-friendly. It is child-friendly, in the language, the prayers, the readings. The active involvement of the children is encouraged. Noise is acceptable!

The difference here is the welcome. The atmosphere is warm. Parents now feel welcome. They feel at home. They start coming to Mass again. It seems such a simple thing, to introduce this participative spirit. And yet it has such an evangelising effect. It has shown its potential to have a significant effect on the faith life of parents and their families.

The weekend Eucharist in general is beginning to adopt this same spirit of welcome. It is moving in this direction, even if too slowly. There is a gradual move away from the culture of 'getting Mass', where Mass is more like a private devotion. There is a growing sense of community, where Mass is shared together. It matters that others are here too! It matters that people are made feel welcome and included. It matters that there is a feeling of community, as opposed to a multiplicity of individuals in the same space.

Eucharist is divine hospitality. We are welcomed by the Lord to the Lord's Table. And the *human* experience of welcome is crucial to it being experienced that way. But we are slow to realise this, slow to appreciate how important the experience of together-ness is. And yet, it is the whole structure of Eucharist. Eucharist is the Word made flesh; bread and wine, body and blood; human and divine. Likewise welcome; the human experience mediates the divine.

How can we move in this direction? There could be greeters at the doors. There could be a 'welcome' banner in different languages. There could be a real sense of 'gathering' and of being welcomed even before Mass begins. Welcome can be part of the priest's words and prayers. There could be a cup of tea afterwards.

Those not present can feel welcome too, through Mass on the parish radio or via the internet, as well as when ministers bring Communion from the Mass to those sick or housebound.

There are two sides to it. Part of it is creating a mood of welcome for those present, and those present opening themselves to the mood of welcome. But also, as the Eucharist becomes a welcoming experience, those gathered can become more aware of their own call to welcome. It is like the prayer above, that all would feel welcomed and called to welcome.

Thus, welcome at Mass is about every member ministry. People step out of the private devotion mode and enter into the spirit of welcome. They come to appreciate their togetherness. As they do, they begin to present a welcoming face to one another. After the Eucharist, they begin to think more about their own ministry of hospitality. In their ordinary everyday lives, people then live their faith in this spirit; with friends, family, neighbours, colleagues – and strangers.

Baptism, First Communion, Confirmation
These three sacraments of initiation are times when the parish's welcoming ministry is to the fore. They are also times of substantial interaction with people who do not frequent church, as well as with those who do. Part of what is significant about these occasions is that evangelisation is happening in the form of welcome.

The word 'initiation' deserves our attention. It means initiation into the Christian faith, three key moments on an individual's faith journey. But it also means initiation into the Christian faith community. People are becoming part of the faith community through these moments. When initiation is seen in that way, we can see how welcome can play such an important role.

Start with Baptism. Increasingly, the focus is on the family having an experience of welcome. In some parishes one of the

Baptism team visits the family, makes them feel comfortable with the process, and then accompanies them as a familiar face at the ceremony. After one ceremony, a mother turned to the Baptism team companion, and said, 'I never realised that Baptism had anything to do with welcome!' The penny had dropped.

In another parish, the process involved being welcomed by the Sunday congregation and participating in sessions with other parents. Afterwards, a mother said that she had come looking for what she called a 'drive-through Baptism', but was delighted with what she had experienced instead. The way we go about Baptism has this potential to be a heart-warming experience of welcome that touches people deep within.

Likewise, today's programmes for First Communion and Confirmation. These are no longer 'provided' by the school alone. They involve the partnership of home, school and parish. The programme of preparation is an interaction with the faith community. The welcome and the involvement of the faith community are transforming the experience of parish for families. For many, more than we realise, it may be the beginning of a new experience of faith and of church.

On these three occasions, many of the parents are not Mass-goers. But, at a very special moment in the life of the family, the programme makes a connection with them. The link is found by many to be uplifting. And welcome is at the heart of it. It helps put parents in touch with the welcoming face of God, as well as with something within that may have been lying dormant.

Experiences of Welcome
Welcome is becoming more significant at funerals too. The funeral team accompanies the families at the church. They help them feel at home and make it comfortable for them taking on roles during

the liturgy. An 'introduction' to the dead person at the start of Mass can give a feeling of welcome to those present who did not directly know the deceased. And some places offer further hospitality with a cup of tea in the parish hall between Mass and burial.

Here, perhaps more than at any other time, most of the people in the church are not churchgoers. Depending on how the occasion is managed, it could leave them unaffected. It could confirm all the reasons they had dismissed church. Or it could be different. Alongside the quality of the prayer and the liturgy, the quality of the welcome can touch people's hearts. It can mediate something of God for them.

All of this so far is about welcome when people come to church. But parishes have also been exploring welcome outside the church. For example, welcoming newcomers to the parish is a particular interest. More and more places are putting together a welcome pack, to give newcomers a warm welcome and a feeling of belonging. There could be a role here for the contact group mentioned in the last chapter, making the parish aware when newcomers have arrived.

More broadly, many parishes have discovered the possibilities in visiting people, be it the whole parish or just a section. The few minutes on the doorstep, the friendly faces, sends out an eloquent message about the welcoming parish. A lot of people feel trepidation at the prospect of visiting; they fear the reaction. But the overwhelming experience has been one of appreciation. The exercise gives people a feeling of welcome and belonging.

Communication is another area with lots of untapped potential. There are many different possibilities for communicating a message of welcome, such as the website, the newsletter, hanging prominent banners outside the church, dropping flyers to people's houses ... This is all about how we put ourselves out there, what we want people to see when they see us. Parishes tend to under-communicate. Yet people notice communication. And welcome is very attractive when we find creative ways of putting it across.

We can also attend to the physical aspect of welcome, to the church building itself. 'Space speaks.' We want those who enter to receive a message of welcome and warmth. I mentioned welcome signs in the porch, but there is more. Those who clean the church, those who arrange the flowers, those who plan the lighting, those who decorate the space for different seasons; all are doing more than just a job. Thanks to them, people who enter feel at home, welcome in God's house.

CHALLENGES

Welcome may sound attractive but it is quite challenging. People warm to the idea but it is not as easy as it might sound at first. In fact, welcome draws us beyond what is familiar, into new and unexplored terrain.

Welcome is a bit like listening. Most people would like to be known as good listeners. Perhaps most people think of themselves as good listeners, but it is probably more accurate to say that most people are not! Likewise, all of us would like to think of our parishes as welcoming places, with a great sense of community. But for all the truth there may be in that, our parishes are not as welcoming as we think.

This recalls the story of the man with the cap. A man arrives at Mass one day wearing a cap, but he does not take it off. One person smiles at him on his way in and reminds him. But he leaves the cap on. During Mass, somebody else taps him on the shoulder and says about the cap. Again he does nothing. Afterwards outside, the priest is meeting people. He comes over and shakes hands. 'I haven't met you before … and I'm curious why you're wearing the cap.' The man replies, 'I've been coming here for two years now, and nobody has ever even said hello to me. But now that I'm wearing the cap, so far three people have spoken to me!' Any parish can see themselves in this story.

Jesus' welcome is boundary-breaking, much more so than ours. Our welcoming spirit often goes only so far. We have blind spots. We have prejudices, including ones that we do not even know we have. We think our welcome is all-embracing – 'of course everyone is welcome here' – until we come up against certain people or certain categories of people. We may be more of a clique than we thought we were.

If we switch to the perspective of the other person, we may be surprised to find there are people out there who do not see us as welcoming. There are some who are thinking, 'Yes, you say that I am welcome to be one of you, but I can see it will mean being less of myself.' There are others who hear the words, but know that we do not know who they are, or what life is like in their shoes. And there are others like the man with the cap!

It comes back again to self-evangelisation, to evangelising ourselves with the Gospel picture. That will lead us, as it did with the theme of care, to open our hearts. It will lead us to look at things from other people's viewpoints. It will help us move from 'making them aware of us' to 'making us aware of them'.

Outside

We must then start to ask: Who is there in this place who might feel like an outsider, outside our faith community? It won't take long before we have a list. For instance, in our parishes there are many 'strangers', just as there were among God's people in the Bible. There are people of other nationalities. There are our own strangers, the travelling people. Often we carry on as though the strangers among us do not exist. But some parishes have gone out of their way to make these 'strangers' feel at home.

143

Another category is people who are 'out of tune' with the church around different church teachings. Many who are gay feel like outsiders; many who are in a second relationship; many who are living together, or not married in church. So much of it is around sexuality. There are many people who feel judged or condemned. There is much suffering in some of these situations. Yet people feel they are being told, 'you are not one of us'.

There is a rarely acknowledged experience of exclusion among women. Patriarchy is still part of our culture, and this may be more true of the church than other places in society. There is the exclusion of women from ministry and from decision-making. There is the reluctance to disown and discard sexist language. It is a man's world, even if many Christian men find that deeply embarrassing. And so, many women have left, while many who stay feel deeply uncomfortable.

A further category is people who ask questions. Yesterday's church was a place of unquestioning obedience. Now we are coming to value 'critical loyalty'. It is possible to belong while having one's own intellectual convictions, not necessarily agreeing with everything. But many questioning people have not heard about that. There is still a sense of a club that demands conformity, rather than a community that values diversity.

Then there are all those people among us who are poor or struggling. Among church people there is a lot of compassion and a lot of generosity towards those who are poor. Yet, from the viewpoint of the poor themselves, it can look like a middle-class church with a middle-class worldview and middle-class concerns.

Again, many young people do not feel that they belong. It looks to them like a church for old people. While people in the church talk a lot about reaching out to young people, often it is about bringing them back on *our* terms, into our kind of church. A young person once asked the question 'When did you ever hear a sermon about young people?'

Then there are those who have stopped going to church for none of these reasons. They may have just drifted. Or else it became irrelevant. Sometimes, especially if it has been a long time, they may feel as if they have burned their boats. They may think that they no longer belong.

The list is not exhaustive. It is indicative of what is out there. There are others whose feelings of not belonging are less obvious. At the same time, we are becoming more aware and more inclusive. Our awareness of people in wheelchairs and of people with impaired hearing are good examples. Another example is where parishes have done something to reach out to the 'strangers' mentioned above.

But it is an ongoing challenge, to become more aware, to see 'from over there', in order to be welcoming in fact and not just in theory. What was said in the last chapter about focus groups and neighbourhood contact groups is also relevant here. These can generate awareness of people for whom a welcome would make all the difference.

Another idea is to make welcome the theme of the parish for the year. Over the year there could be a variety of well-chosen projects. Part of this would be good communication with the faith community, bringing everybody in on the theme. One outcome from the year might be that more people would feel welcome. Another might be that more people become aware of their call to welcome, their every member ministry.

In conclusion, there is a new sense of welcome in our parishes. This encourages us to embrace challenges like those just listed. Ultimately we know that, as we grow more welcoming, we are at the same time discovering in an ever more joyful way what it means to be church.

Chapter Twelve
Listening

To be an evangelising parish means being a caring parish. It means being a welcoming parish. And it means being a listening parish. Listening is a form of evangelising and being evangelised. It too is a part of every member ministry. We will begin by reflecting on how this theme emerges from the direction of the previous chapters. There are four aspects to this.

FOUR ASPECTS

First, the discussion of both care and welcome highlighted awareness. The evangelising parish seeks to make 'us more aware of them', more aware of who is out there, in order to find out *how* to be welcoming and caring. Listening is how we become more aware of who is out there. We become aware of people's suffering. We become aware of needs, great and small.

Second, the 'who's who' chapter discussed the change from a clerical church to a people's church. In the clerical church, 'lay' people's experience was one of silence. But a people's church is participative. The life experience and inner wisdom of each one matter. The views and feelings of each one matter. The style of spirituality of each one matters. But because people's experience has been one of silence, they are not used to talking or being invited to think. It takes time to cultivate a culture of listening.

Third, in the early chapters we reflected on what is going on 'out there'. We spoke about God's Spirit being active in people's lives outside the church. This too points to a listening that is needed. People 'in here' are called to appreciate what is going on in the spiritual lives of people 'out there'. They are called to open themselves to that richness; to learn, to be enriched, to be challenged.

Fourth, the idea of we ourselves being evangelised is a major dimension of the evangelising parish. Evangelisation begins by opening ourselves to being evangelised by the Gospel. In this way too, listening is fundamental in tomorrow's faith community. That community listens to the Word, to Scripture. The listening is ongoing, a never-ending matter of being re-amazed again and again by what we believe.

On the one hand there is listening to people; to members of the faith community, to others beyond that community, to the situation of others still whom we are not aware of. On the other hand there is listening to the Word. We will elaborate on each of these, with ideas on how to go about listening.

LISTENING TO PEOPLE

I will outline a number of ways in which the parish can listen to people. In considering any particular approach, it is important to ask three questions: Who? Why? What next? First we ask; who will we be listening to? We want to listen to people who go to church and we want to listen to people who do not. Different methods reach different audiences.

Second, we ask; what is the purpose of the listening? It could be for our own sake; to gather information, to learn, to help us plan. Or the aim could be about the people we are listening to. It could be to give them a voice. It could be to share experience. It could be for the experience itself of being listened to. If so, the process itself may be more valuable than any outcome.

Third, we think ahead to what comes next. If we listen, we are also committing ourselves to taking on board what we hear. Therefore, some follow-up is usually part of the process. If so, it needs to be built in from the start. Some listening is for its own sake, complete in itself. Other listening is only complete when there is a response. Without that, people may wonder if they were really listened to at all.

Survey

One form of listening is to carry out a census-like survey in order to ascertain just who is living in the parish. With the help of census figures we can work up a 'profile' of the population in the parish area. We find out the age profile of the parish, socio-economic groupings, and so on. We can compare the profile with what goes on currently. Is our parish and its activities geared to the population living here? In this way, listening feeds into planning.

Suggestion Box

Here, a box is placed at each entrance to the church (possibly in other locations in the parish also), with pens and paper alongside. The question or questions being asked can be displayed on a notice, as well as on the reply forms. The initiative and the reasons for it can be introduced to people at Mass, as well as in the newsletter and on the website.

The choice of questions deserves time and thought. It could be something general, for instance, 'What might our faith community concentrate its energies on over the next few years?' Or the question could be more specific, for instance, 'What do you find most satisfying/frustrating about the Mass you go to?' Or, 'Mention one way in which our parish could be more welcoming.'

This listening, obviously, is limited to those who go to church and amounts to no more than a modest engagement with people. But it has its uses. It puts out a message about wanting to listen. What fruit it bears depends a lot on how well it is presented to people. Also, if something emerges and is seen to be addressed, straight away the usefulness of listening has shot up in people's estimation.

Questionnaires

The heading is plural because questionnaires can take different forms. The most familiar is when the questionnaire is either left in the church or put in letterboxes. Another option is to call to people with the questionnaire, explain it, then call back to collect it later. Usually, the purpose of such questionnaires is to gather people's views about what is going on in the parish and what is needed.

This idea has its ups and downs. There is almost always a low rate of return. The anonymity makes it easy for people to criticise or to throw things back on the parish. There will be people saying, 'what you should be doing is ...' There will be people venting about their hobby horses. But those are just the downsides, and are inevitable. If it is carefully prepared, with a clear aim in mind and well presented to the parish, a questionnaire can provide useful data. A lot of the feedback will be predictable. But if some action results, people will have a sense of being listened to.

Another possibility is handing out a questionnaire during Sunday Mass. For example, I was once involved in a survey about adult faith. It had been explained to the congregation the previous Sunday that there would be a questionnaire the next week. After a homily on the topic, pens and paper were handed out. The page listed possible ways of enriching adult faith, such as: how to pray; exploring Scripture; nourishment for parents; faith and justice; one's own spiritual journey. People numbered off their preferences.

About 750 replies came in, and a very clear picture of people's own perceived needs emerged. This shows the potential for other topics too. In a very simple but structured way, the exercise recovers high quality feedback from a large number of people. It gets people reflecting on themselves and their parish, and makes for a follow-through that is a practical response to felt needs.

A variant on this is to devote the homilies for a few weekends to reflections on a theme such as 'Parish, today and tomorrow' or 'Will our children have faith?' There are pens and paper on the final day, for people to respond to what they have heard over the few weeks. There could also be a short gathering after the Mass, to share and to gather people's reactions and responses.

Listening to Ministry Groups

Listening to those involved in ministries has two purposes. Part of it is for the groups themselves. It is a form of acknowledgment. They are asked about their experience, how they are getting on, what needs they have. They are invited to make observations, based on their ministry, about where things are at in the parish and what needs a response. The session(s) could also incorporate an element of enrichment for those taking part, to deepen their spirituality.

The other part of it is for the parish. Listening helps the parish evaluate how the groups are getting on and what needs to be improved. It helps identify gaps in what is being addressed in the parish. It helps planning. But maybe most of all, it brings many more voices in on conversations about where the parish is at and what the priorities for planning should be.

There are different ways of carrying out this listening. Groups could be met with one by one, or they could meet in clusters, all those involved in related ministries coming together. Or they could be brought together in one large gathering, where there is a mix of ministries. Each has its own merits. Again there are the two outcomes: collecting feedback for planning, and people feeling listened to.

Sharing Experience
One shared experience that comes to mind here is the way people in some parishes came together in the context of the child sexual abuse scandals. They came to articulate their feelings and share in their faith at such a difficult time for the church. Another is when some parishes organised discussion sessions to gather responses to the Vatican questionnaires for the 2014 and 2015 synods on the family.

Regarding the latter, some people commented that it was the first time they had ever been consulted by the church about anything! And that is the point. In the past, the 'laity' were silent. And it was not just silence regarding their views. Their experience was also silent. I think again of all the parents in the last number of decades who have had to come to terms with their own sons and daughters not going to church. How many opportunities were offered to share their feelings, to help them deal positively with the situation?

There is something about ownership here. Tomorrow's parish is a place where people talk, where their feelings matter, where their views are valued. A parish without conversation is going to be no more than a service-parish, just like the provided-for parish of the past. A participative parish is one that is for 'hearing people into speech'. It is one where public opinion is valued. This is part of every member ministry.

Informal Listening
These next two ideas came up in the chapter on care. One way to get people involved in informal listening is to gather a small group of people, and train them for this simple exercise. The idea

is that they will have a facilitated weekly meeting for four weeks or so. In between each meeting they will listen to people. They will not do anything different from usual, except to listen informally, with a heightened awareness. They will give more of their attention to what people are talking about in places like shops, schoolyards, bus stops, clinics, pubs, and so on.

In particular they will listen for what people are talking most passionately about. They will listen for what is full of feeling; anger or anxiety, worry or hope, delight and joy, confusion and threat. The group members note what they hear and share this when they meet. Through them, the parish is listening to what matters to people. As patterns emerge, the parish can move to the next step of identifying possible ways of connecting with people.

Focus Group
When it comes to focus groups, the group has some common denominator, and is more introspective. It could, for example, be a group of young people, people from the same area, parents of young children, bereaved people, etc. Their focus is on people who have a similar life experience to themselves. They might begin by sharing their own life experience and observations. What is life like for people like us? What are our hopes and fears? Where do we find God in our lives?

The next step would be as above; informal but heightened listening to people like themselves. When they gather to share, they can also compare what they heard to what they had shared themselves. As the conversation develops, what is emerging is a kind of 'like-to-like' ministry. People are discerning meeting points between the world of people like themselves and the Good News of the Gospel.

A Listening Theme
The idea here is that listening would be presented as the focus of

the whole parish for, say, the next six months. There would be a lot of publicity. There could be homilies presenting the project. It would be a regular part of prayer at Mass. Different listening exercises from the above might be planned.

At the heart of it would be the weekly celebration of Eucharist. In the spirit of every member ministry, the aim would be to engage as many as possible with the theme. All would be encouraged to be listeners on behalf of their faith community. They would bring this listening to prayer at the weekly Eucharist. They would pray for those whom they have become aware of. There could be a 'prayer basket' where people could write something based on what they had heard. Occasionally, perhaps in a brief, focused meeting after Mass, there could be a chance for people to share what they have heard.

Parish Assembly
I have left this way of listening until last, even though it may be one of the more familiar ones, my reason being that it may also be left until the end of any listening process embarked on by the parish. In other words, it could be the culminating point, where other smaller listening projects converge.

Parish assemblies have different purposes, such as a parish celebration or a parish anniversary. Often they include an element of discerning needs and identifying priorities, perhaps with the help of a specially prepared prayer and an inspirational talk. There could be anything from 50 to 200 people turning up, depending on the kind of publicity and promotion that goes into it, as well as on the size of the parish.

In such an assembly, the only people teasing out needs and priorities are those present, usually the core churchgoers and people involved in ministries. Their perspective is valuable, but it is also limited. If the parish is thinking about outreach, then other voices need to be heard as well. This highlights the advantage of the assembly coming at the end of a process of listening in the parish.

When it is timed in that way, the assembly already has material to work on. It is not depending just on what comes up on the day. The assembly begins by listening to the listening that has already been going on. It moves from there into a moment of discernment. It seeks to hear what the Spirit is saying to the community. It seeks to discern the path on which it is being invited to travel.

As well as the ideas mentioned, there is also the idea of having facilitated area gatherings, or even house gatherings. This would be a big operation and a big effort of organisation would be required. People would be meeting in smaller, local groups to share their feelings about the parish and about faith today. But were it to happen, it would be a big energy feeding into an assembly.

LISTENING TO THE WORD

The Christian, it has been said, is somebody who carries a Bible in one hand and a newspaper in the other. Christians are people who listen deeply on both fronts. They listen intently to the Word, the Gospel, and they listen attentively to the world around them. They then relate the two to one another. They bring life to Scripture and Scripture to life. When we bring life – our own life and the world around us – with us as we listen to the Word, we are then listening to the Word in our context, not in a vacuum. This makes it possible to hear new meanings in the Bible that we might not otherwise have picked up. In this way, life helps reveal and open up the fuller meaning of the Word.

And when we bring Scripture and our listening to the Word to our lives, that also is revealing. Our listening to the Word enables us to listen to life – our own life and the world around us – with new ears. We see our world differently, from a Gospel perspective. New meanings open up to us. Thus, listening to the Word and listening to the world throw light on one another.

Listening to the Word in this way is for everybody in the faith community. It is every member ministry. Each person is called to be a 'minister of the Word' in this sense. Each one listens to the Word. Each one listens to the world and to what is going on in people's lives. And then each one can also speak a word; a word of hope, a word of joy, a word of comfort. Each one can evangelise.

Learning to Listen

People in parishes are generally quite unfamiliar with the Bible and unused to reading or praying with it. Some have developed a relationship with Scripture, but it is not widespread. What follows are three suggestions for helping people develop a relationship with Scripture. Chapter seven noted the challenge here.

First, there is a real need to attend to the Liturgy of the Word at Sunday Eucharist. It needs to be less a case of 'words, words, words', which often go over people's heads or fail to connect. It needs to become an *experience* of the Word, an occasion when the Word enters into people's hearts, where it enlightens their minds, where it resonates with their lives, where it connects with where they are at, where it speaks to their world.

An ideal scenario might be along the following lines. Before Mass begins, a minister of the Word welcomes people with a sentence presenting the theme of the liturgy. There is a pause before the first reading, inviting people into a listening disposition. The homily is focused on linking the Scripture with people's lives. The Prayers of the Faithful flow from this, and include intercessions about our lives inspired by the Word we have listened to.

After Communion there might be a final brief reflection on the Word. As people leave, there could be a simple hand-out with an excerpt from the day's Scripture on it, plus a reflection – and perhaps the text of the intercessions – as a 'word of life' for people to take with them into the week ahead.

That is an ideal. With a concerted effort, it does not seem too difficult to raise the profile of the Liturgy of the Word and to draw people into a deeper engagement with the Word. There is a role for the ministers of the Word here. Their 'job description' can be expanded beyond 'doing a reading'. They could come to see themselves as facilitating familiarity with the Word among the faith community – a further ministry they might be ideally suited for.

Second, building on this, the faith community can encourage its members to enter into the practice of reading Scripture, especially the gospels. A thought from Pope Francis illustrates this perfectly;

> We, as Jesus' disciples, are called upon to be people who listen to His voice and take His words seriously … It is a good idea to have a small Gospel, a pocket-sized Gospel that you can carry around with you, and to read a short passage from it at any time of the day. At any time in the day I take the Gospel out of my pocket and read a little something, a short passage. There we find Jesus.[30]

The parish could make pocket gospels available. People can also be encouraged to download a Bible app on their smartphones, so they can have the whole Bible with them all the time. The parish could build from this by offering help and resources in learning the art of reading the Bible meditatively (known as *lectio divina*).

Third, developing familiarity with Scripture could also be done by way of small groups. These groups might resemble the 'basic Christian communities' that flourish in some parts of the world.

In them, people come together in gatherings to relate the Word to life. They listen to the Word. They share the concerns of their lives. They bring life to Scripture, and Scripture to life. There is also the possibility of study groups, where people can learn more about the Bible.

CROSSING OVER

The parish listens to people and people listen to the Word. Most of it will sound quite new, unfamiliar in that sense. It is also unfamiliar in another sense. It is like crossing the border from where we are into the territory of God. Listening has something of this about it, a crossing over from where we are comfortable and on familiar ground.

This is the case when we listen to people 'out there', who are not churchgoers. It is the case when we listen to people 'in here', who may not have had a voice before. It is the case when we listen in order to become aware of people we have not noticed. And it is the case when we listen anew to the Word. In each case we are venturing into the unfamiliar. In each case we are entering into holy ground. Each crossing over has the potential to surprise us, to enrich us.

In this way, listening is a dimension of the evangelising parish and how it expresses itself. It expresses itself when people listen to the Word and when people feel listened to themselves. In the process, the parish itself is being evangelised. And people are being facilitated into every member ministry, where they become evangelisers themselves.

CHAPTER THIRTEEN
Praying

It might be true to say that, in the past, parish was mainly about prayer. Parish life and activity revolved largely around the sacraments and various forms of prayer or devotion. As such, there is nothing novel about highlighting prayer. But the evangelising parish is about discovering prayer in new ways, in new forms appropriate to the challenges of its new situation.

The last chapter observed how the Liturgy of the Word can often be 'words, words, words'. But, since the changes of Vatican II, prayer in the parish can be 'Mass, Mass, Mass'. The older parish was blessed with a variety of different prayer occasions. People came together for benediction, for the rosary, for sodalities, for adoration, for novenas. There were special prayers for times during the year, such as when visiting the church on All Souls' Day, and for the Corpus Christi procession.

The 'rediscovery' of Mass – when it was translated into the people's own language – had a downside, as much of the previous variety of ways of praying was lost. Then came a new kind of routine, with a Mass for practically every occasion. Eventually, it ended up that there were too many Masses and not enough prayer. Sometimes, when there is a non-Eucharistic ritual that touches people's lives, we sense this. And, not infrequently, the 'celebration' of Sunday Eucharist can feel more like going through the motions, lacking a mood of prayer.

Things are changing though. New occasions for prayer apart from Eucharist have been emerging, and there have been new initiatives to revitalise the celebration of the Eucharist itself. This chapter reflects on these two expressions of the evangelising parish and the many opportunities there are for prayer.

On the one hand, the evangelising parish is engaged in creating experiences of prayer that connect with people at important moments in their lives. On the other, it is engaged in renewing and transforming the experience of Eucharist for those who gather. In the first case, the parish is more focused on creating evangelising moments for people 'out there'. In the second it is more about the need for people 'in here' to be evangelised.

PRAYER OCCASIONS

We will start with prayer, ritual and liturgy outside of the Eucharist. Tomorrow's parish will be giving this a lot of attention as a form of outreach and evangelisation. It will be reaching out particularly to people who no longer have much contact with church. But, obviously, the ideas described here are for churchgoers too.

As already noted, people who stop going to church do not stop praying. When the parish seeks to connect with them through occasions of prayer, it is building on the prayerfulness or spirituality that is there by offering something that many cannot provide for themselves. It offers a language for expressing religious experience. It offers ritual for engaging with life events at a spiritual depth. It offers community and support.

Sometimes we talk of 'bringing them back', of getting people back to Mass. But that may be further down the line. For people who are baptised but not connected with church, Eucharist may come at the *end* of a process of re-engagement. Maybe care and welcome come first, helping reconnect with the faith community. And prayer occasions are part of that, part of feeling noticed and welcomed and cared for.

Death

Death comes first to mind when thinking about how the parish engages with people at a key moment in their lives. The main prayer occasions are the funeral rituals and liturgies in the church. In terms of attendance, they are becoming the biggest liturgies that happen in the church. And yet, they are also the occasions with the highest number of people present who do not otherwise go to church.

'Outreach' suggests physically going somewhere. But in this case, the people come to us. The outreach is in our hearts; it is spiritual. It is in how we prepare for and manage the occasion. We need to offer the ritual from a mentality of reaching out. The ritual is then shaped by our knowledge of who is present. We take them into account. This is qualitatively very different from just doing what we always did, or just following the texts.

The role here of funeral teams goes beyond filling a gap as the number of priests diminishes. They are involved in evangelising. Their aim is for people to feel a warmth of welcome and a sense of belonging. Their hope is that people will take with them a sense of having been in a sacred space of praying, of having connected with something 'more'.

It is not just the team, though. It is every member. Everyone goes to funerals. At any funeral, many are neighbours from the parish and many visitors are churchgoers themselves. They too have a ministry; they are more than just a congregation. The way they participate, in prayer and singing, can help others participate and can communicate hospitality. The parish can encourage this ministry by talking about it and making its members more aware of it. In some parishes the weekday Mass community has grown into such a role.

Welcome is also relevant to the tensions around eulogies and the presentation of gifts. There is frustration over what seem like 'secular events in sacred settings'. There is an element here of non-churchgoing people, at a moment of deep feeling, wanting to ritualise from within themselves. Welcome takes the form of an accommodation on both sides. But non-Eucharistic funerals are also part of the way forward. They are going to be more frequent anyway, but they also allow more scope for creativity.

Of course, there are other occasions apart from funerals. In November, visiting the church on All Souls' Day used to be big. Today we have special liturgies in church during the month for all who are bereaved, especially those who have lost someone in the last year. It is a real example of offering something distinctive. The faith community offers structure, language, ritual, support for people. It notices them. It welcomes them. These liturgies can be quite creative, touching people at a deep level. And they also give us an inkling of what is possible.

A prayer card for the anniversary of death is an eloquent way for the parish to think of the bereaved and to communicate a sense of others praying for them. Again, the annual Mass or ritual at the graveyard or cemetery is a cherished occasion for all, an opportunity for people to bring their feelings into a place of prayer.

Parishes have also hosted rituals for parents who have lost a child, through stillbirth or miscarriage, or through tragedy after birth. Parishes have hosted rituals for people who are suffering after losing a loved one through a suicide. Again, people are being noticed. In the outreach, care and prayer come together.

Family Prayer
The family rosary is remembered by older people with feelings ranging from fondness and nostalgia to ones that are a lot less positive, such as boredom and compulsion. The thing is, however,

that the rosary has not been replaced. There is a gap, an absence of family prayer. It is a major area for the evangelising parish to address, to facilitate the adoption of new ways of praying together as a family.

It is easiest to introduce when the family is very young. Baptism is a good starting point. For example, the family could be presented with an attractive prayer card. Each evening, the parents bless their baby on the forehead, saying the blessing prayer on the card. This is very simple, non-threatening, yet very real and intimate.

When children are a little older, the family could pray at meal times to thank God for the food they are about to eat, and at bedtime in a prayer of thanks for the day. A prayer card could help here too. Again it is easy and simple. And the children may well be the leaders, easing parents into it. It can soon become a cherished part of the day. Recalling that Eucharist means thanksgiving, the daily prayer of thanks is Eucharistic in its own way.

At Lent and Advent, the parish can offer further resources. A special prayer card for the season, together with a candle, could be distributed at Mass. People could take extra for neighbours or friends. Or there could be a candle and prayer for November, for remembering grandparents or other fond friends who have died.

Blessing of homes is another idea. Many young families have never done this. A team of people could be trained to visit those who are interested, and to carry out the ritual. An attractive prayer card could be printed for the occasion, and the children can be involved in the prayers. A gift from the parish could be included, such as a holy water font, an icon, or a copy of the New Testament. This could be an opportunity to offer resources for family prayer.

It is an area really worth exploring. Bringing up a family is such a huge part of so many people's lives. They may not use the language of religion, but what they are doing is deeply spiritual.

The parish can help make connections between life and faith by making available its resources; its language, its rituals, its care and support. For the parents, this can be a step on the path to every member ministry, supporting them as faith-companions in the lives of their children.

Healing

The theme of healing brings together some further possibilities. Special liturgies and prayers have been developed around World Day of the Sick, and the Sacrament of Anointing can be celebrated communally as part of this. There could be other occasions during the year when people are invited to experience the ritual as well. Another outreach is the way many parishes involve Ministers of the Eucharist in bringing Communion to the sick, after Sunday Mass, on the first Friday, or at other times.

The Sacrament of Reconciliation links with the need for spiritual and relational healing. The communal form still has untapped potential and is in need of revitalisation. Maybe it needs to be more communal, with a more creative ritual, and perhaps something like general absolution or general confession. One possibility is to offer it to parents on the occasion of their children's first confession.

The rituals that were organised in some churches and parishes around the issue of child sexual abuse illustrate the way in which a particular need for healing is responded to and ritualised. The parish can learn to be sensitive to times of particular suffering, be it close to home or further afield, when special rituals could be offered.

Key Moments

There are great ideas and rich resources in a book called *Parish Rituals for Key Moments*, by Eileen Deegan.[31] It provides over twenty different rituals for prayer occasions outside of Mass.

Some of them relate to ideas mentioned above; rituals for funerals, for reconciliation, for November, for blessing a home, for parents who have lost a child, for people bereaved by suicide.

The collection also includes rituals for expectant parents; for parents whose child is beginning school; for those sitting exams. There are rituals of affirmation for people who build community, and for teachers. There are rituals for different times of the year: for St Brigid's Day; for Valentine's Day; for Mothers' Day; for Fathers' Day; for Grandparents' Day; for Harvest. There is a Sundown Service for the end of the year.

The book also includes a ritual of Confirmation outside Mass, and there is another for parents who have had a child baptised during the year. Again, at these key moments in family life, creative prayer occasions can link faith and life. They can help articulate the spiritual meaning of what is going on for people. They can open a door on the sacred.

Preparation for the Sacraments of Initiation has developed impressively in recent years. The programmes include new forms of ritual: the service of light before Confirmation; a preparation Mass or ritual before First Communion; a welcome Mass for families ahead of Baptism. Another idea, bridging between Baptism and First Communion, is an annual blessing for children under First Communion age.

Marriage can also be seen as part of our Christian initiation. There could be a ritual to celebrate anniversaries, or to renew promises. In a spirit of welcome, this could include all couples, not just those married in church. There could be a Mass for engaged couples, to celebrate their love and build a feeling of belonging.

Flexibility is a key characteristic of such rituals. They can be part of Mass, but more often they stand alone. They can take place in different locations, not just church, but also in the school, in a prayer room, in the home. It is not about people coming to our liturgies, but our rituals coming to people's lives. It is about paying attention to what matters in people's lives and then responding imaginatively, sensitively, creatively.

Visibility

There are many other ideas too, such as: parish missions, triduums and novenas; directed prayer and spiritual direction; meditation and *lectio divina*; Taizé prayer; adoration in the church; different styles of prayer group. All this indicates the numerous possibilities for the evangelising parish – sensitive awareness of these helps the parish get in touch with the needs in the faith community. Creativity and imagination make for prayer experiences that can connect deeply and nourish the spirit.

In the process, a new image of parish comes into view. Parish can now be seen as more than just a building where people go for occasional services. It is more than just Mass. It becomes 'visible' to people as a place of prayer. It becomes known as a place in touch with mystery and in touch with people in their spiritual need. It is a 'go-to' place for meeting God. People come to feel that 'we care that you exist'.

EUCHARIST

Eucharist is central to the faith community. Because of its importance, there needs to be a commitment to excellence, both spiritually and practically. There needs to be a commitment to enhancing the occasion; to deepening the experience of Eucharist as the heart, the source, the high point, the inspiration of the community. If Eucharist is routine, we are out of touch with ourselves. Celebrating Eucharist and being evangelised go hand in hand.

Chapter three talked about the plus and minus of current practice. There is the new mood, and there is the new mode of participation. We now talk of 'celebrating the Eucharist'. But what we do often leaves a lot to be desired. It can be routine, lifeless, joyless, lacking togetherness, even lacking prayer. This is partly a relic of the 'getting Mass' culture.

So Eucharist today is between states, between 'getting Mass' and 'celebrating Eucharist'. There is a spectrum in the quality of what goes on. The question this raises is not about how to bring people back to Mass. The question is: back to what? How do we ourselves see what we are doing? Are we getting Mass or are we celebrating Eucharist? What is the mood? What is the quality of prayer? What is the quality of togetherness? What is the quality of engagement and participation?

Vertical and Horizontal

How do we see what we are doing? I will answer this in two ways. The first is with the image of vertical and horizontal. 'Vertical' refers to the divine dimension, the God-focus of the Eucharist. 'Horizontal' refers to the human dimension, the community focus of the Eucharist. We need to see Eucharist as a balance of both.

People talk of Mass being their special quiet time during the week. This is a vertical perspective, seeing it as time spent in God's presence, time for reflection, prayer, contemplation. Others, conditioned by the old Latin Mass, may also have a vertical focus. The distance that was created in the old Mass made it almost a private devotion, between the individual and God. And the conditioning lingers on.

But the very meaning of Eucharist demands an equally strong horizontal perspective. The Eucharist is a *gathering*. It is not a collection of individuals; it is the body of Christ. There has to be a real togetherness about it. Much more is needed than a sign of peace towards the end of the proceedings. Earlier, describing 'faith in the heart', we saw that belonging is an essential dimension of faith. If togetherness is weak, the Lord can feel less than 'really present'.

In the horizontal dimension, the following are some ways in which to build a sense of togetherness:

❖ A sense of community from the start. It should feel more like arriving at a party than at a cinema. Encourage people to come earlier. Greet them at the door. Go through the music. Shake hands with those alongside you. Welcome people warmly.

❖ Singing creates community, so a serious effort should be made to get people joining in at key moments in the liturgy. A cantor may be needed to make this happen.

❖ The homily can generate a sense of togetherness around a theme that is relevant, life-giving, hopeful, encouraging, and challenging.

❖ The presentation of the gifts can highlight our presentation of ourselves. We who are gathered are ourselves part of the transformation into the body of Christ.

❖ A word around Communion time to highlight the point that, in receiving, we become the body of Christ, and are now called to live as his body.

❖ A cup of tea afterwards, as a chance to mingle.

Turning to the vertical dimension, the following are some ways in which to create a mood of prayer.[32]

❖ Moments of silence are key to a mood of prayer. These can be extremely brief: a focusing moment at the start; a pause before the Liturgy of the Word; a moment's quiet after the homily; a moment to think of one's own intentions during the Prayer of the Faithful; a reflective moment at the presentation of the gifts; meditation time after Communion. They interrupt the tendency to drift or daydream. They bring people into a place of contemplation, into a shared space of silence.

❖ The quality of the homily. In *The Joy of the Gospel* Francis devotes twelve pages to this! 'A preacher has to contemplate the Word, but he also has to contemplate his people ... He needs to be able to link the message of a biblical text to a human situation.'[33] The homily then brings people into a place of prayer.

❖ The Prayer of the Faithful. Instead of being mechanical, predictable and clichéd, the intercessions should be capable of inspiring further prayer in people's hearts.

❖ The music. While the main focus in music is the participation of the assembly, there is an important role for the choir – performing. The quality of these pieces has the potential to lift people heavenwards, to connect with mystery.

Four Moments
How do we see what we are doing? My first answer is to see it as both vertical and horizontal. The second is to see what we are doing as made up of four moments. These are: Gathering; Word; Eucharist; and Sending.[34]

Mass, we know, used to be a private devotion for most people. Part of that old experience was that everything was reduced to one moment – the consecration. As we saw it, that was what priests were ordained for and that was what people came for. The congregation were akin to spectators. They were prayerful, but they were looking on, as something extraordinary happened up there on the altar at the hands of the priest.

Everything else in the Mass was effectively devalued. People could arrive at the creed and leave after the priest received

Communion; and they would have done enough to have 'got Mass'. No gathering, no Word, no Communion, no sending. It was as if these were all trimmings. We are still in the process of entering into a four-moment Eucharist. This, together with the balancing of vertical and horizontal, accounts for the variety in the quality of what people experience.

There has already been some reference to these moments above. The chapter on faith in the heart, the head and the hands spoke about them. The chapter on listening reflected on the Word. In the chapter on welcoming (and again above) we spoke about the gathering moment. But all four matter. If any is weak or neglected, then the Eucharist is not being fully celebrated.

The gathering and sending moments are perhaps most vulnerable to neglect, because they are such short moments. When we invite people to a party, we say '7.30 for 8.00'. Sometimes that half-hour is the best part. But people arrive at the last minute for Mass. Again, we need to push for people to come earlier. We need to be working on a feeling of gathering. How we begin sets the tone. We should start as we mean to go on.

Likewise, the conclusion of Mass needs to be more like a sending than an ending. 'The Mass is ended / thanks be to God' ... it can feel like 'that's it done for another week'. There should be a strong concluding focus, like when we speak of somebody getting a great send-off. The entire celebration should be gathered into this moment where we depart with a feeling of unity and a feeling of mission.

Weekdays

Weekday Mass in the parish may well hold the best balance of horizontal and vertical. There is a strong sense of community; people miss you when you are not in your usual place! With less priests there will be less weekday Masses. Yet that community remains. What we do in that situation depends, again, on being able to see things differently.

170

If Mass is all about the consecration, then people are going to be thinking in terms of some kind of Communion service. If we cannot have Mass, they say, at least we can have Communion. The theology in that understanding of Eucharist falls short. The way to go is to have a service of the Word instead of Eucharist, led by trained parishioners. There would be a focus on the prayerful reading of Scripture and on prayers that link Scripture with life.[35]

This would be another creative, non-Eucharistic ritual. There is real potential here for this group of parishioners to enter into a deeper relationship with the Word. That in turn would feed into Sunday Eucharist. A core of people would already be attuned to this type of celebration, leading the way where more could follow, thereby promoting an enhanced Liturgy of the Word.

CHAPTER FOURTEEN
Family

Family has been a recurrent theme in the last few chapters, sometimes quite explicit, other times less so. This chapter brings family into sharper focus, at the centre of the life of the evangelising parish. It is included in this new edition of the book, in the year of the World Meeting of Families in Dublin.

It was remarked earlier that most of the new life-giving initiatives in parishes in recent times have had a lot to do with welcome. Welcome has emerged as a 'signature' quality of tomorrow's parish. Looking again at those initiatives, it can also be observed how many of them have to do with family. Think of the family Mass; of the ministry of Baptism teams; of bereavement ministry and funeral teams; of annual parish 'family fun' days; of programmes for First Communion and Confirmation. Family is at the heart of it all.

If that is so – if family is so prominent in the vitality in today's parish – then that is an invitation to deeper reflection. We are invited to delve deeper, to explore the depths of the link between 'parish' and 'family'

Structures and Activities

First, we will pause to think about the word 'family'. We will leave aside for the moment phrases like the 'Holy Family' and the 'Catholic Family' and simply think about the word family today. What I want to highlight is the shift there has been, from thinking of family as a structure to thinking about family in terms of activities.

In the past, family was understood as a structure, an institution, a central institution in the structure of society. When people married, they entered into an institutional set-up. The institution was there mainly for the raising of children. Love between the partners was not centre-stage like it is today. There were even 'arranged marriages'. There was the phrase, 'love ends when marriage begins'.

The structure comprised father, mother, sons and daughters. We recall remarks about a 'Protestant' family having one son and one daughter and a 'Catholic' family having many of both. But it is the same structure. There was an implication that anything less was less than what 'family' was meant to be. A childless couple; a single-parent; a broken marriage; a second relationship – and more recently, a gay couple – it was as if the description 'family' did not sit quite as well there.

Today, people think about family more in terms of activities than in terms of structure. What are the core activities that go on in a family? What would family members – partners, parents, children – say in answer to that question? Each of us can think of our own words. The words would most likely include love, acceptance, care, security, support, belonging, fun, togetherness, sharing, forgiveness, understanding – and many more. Such words capture that heart of what family is about.

We can see immediately how *inclusive* such language is. Thinking of family as a structure tends to be exclusive. Those who do not fit the traditional definition can feel that they are less, that they are 'outside'. But thinking of activities is more all-embracing. Different situations are incorporated. Family comes in different shapes and sizes and all can see them themselves as 'family', as insiders.

Of course structures matter, not for their own sake but for the sake of the activities. Some set-ups are less conducive than others and all want the set-up that best facilitates the activities that 'family' is all about. The point I am making is the value of focusing on the activities and how inclusive this is.

There is more to it. A focus on the activities also opens up other links that are exciting and hope-filled. A focus on activities links family with Gospel and links family with church/parish in ways that will repay exploration.

Family, Parish, Gospel
Jean Vanier said that 'the fundamental principle of all education is to open the heart and the mind to the needs of others'. It consists in 'helping people discover all that is positive and beautiful within themselves, and to realise that they can establish relationships with others, that they are loveable and able to love'[36].

Vanier is expressing very eloquently what being a human being is about, what human becoming is all about. This brings out the deep meaning of the activities that go on in the family. When there are security and belonging, togetherness and care, and so on – the activities alluded to above – that is the environment where people discover their humanity, where they enter into their humanity.

This brings to mind a couple of phrases from the documents of Vatican II. There, family is described as 'the school of human enrichment' and as 'the school of social virtues'[37]. 'Education' literally means 'leading out' and the family is a school in this sense. It draws out what is within the person, so that people are enriched in their humanity. 'Social virtues' means that it draws out the capacity and the qualities for relating with others, for thinking 'we' and not just 'me', for discovering that we are most human when we are other-centred.

Seen in this light, family is perhaps the most person-making environment that there is. So much so that the same documents of Vatican II added that its 'educational' function is next to irreplaceable. It is almost impossible to provide an adequate substitute.

All of this resonates strikingly with some reflections from earlier in this book. In chapter six, we made links between what goes on in the parish and what is going on in the gospels. The links led us to say that the parish is meant to 'earth' the Gospel, to be the 'today' of the activities going on in the Gospel. Now we can add to the picture. It is not only the parish that is meant to earth the Gospel; so is the family. The core activities in all three – family, Gospel, parish – are very similar. This gives a uniquely Christian perspective on the family.

A brief recall of chapter six will help. The words welcome and compassion capture much of what Jesus was about, the core activities he engaged in. Through the experience of his care and of feeling included, people rediscover their humanity. His understanding, his healing, his forgiveness rekindle hope and release the love locked within.

In this, even more than in his words, Jesus 'speaks' of God. Like an artist, he 'portrays' God, as the God of welcome and compassion towards each and every one. In the experience of his resurrection, his companions come to see that, in portraying God, he incarnates God.

Parish, the presence of 'church' in a particular place, is meant to earth this for today. The local Christian community is asked to imitate Jesus, through its welcome and inclusion and community, through its caring and compassion. As it does, it too 'portrays' to people the God of Jesus Christ. It too 'speaks' the Good News about God and about ourselves.

Family speaks a very similar language. It too is meant to be a warm and welcoming space, a place of security and belonging, acceptance and enrichment. Amidst the ups and downs of daily life, the sense of caring and being cared for is fundamental. In this again, people are imitating Jesus; they are portraying the God of Jesus. This is the challenge of being family, the possibility, the deep meaning.

So, what is going on in the family, what is going on in the gospels and what is going on in the parish are very much along the same lines. We will draw out what this means by proposing, on the one hand, that 'church' is a word for family and, on the other, that 'family' is a word for church or parish.

'Church' – a Word for Family
First, what might it mean to say that 'church' is a word for family, an image for family, throwing light on what it means to be a family? The answer is already present in what we have been saying.

If the activities in both are similar, then in some sense family *is* church. Activities such as welcoming, accepting, building community, caring and forgiving are at the heart of both family and church. They are at the heart of church because they are the heart of the Gospel, the activities flowing from the heart of Jesus. If the core of the family is the same activities, then family is itself what church is called to be.

Traditionally, this has been expressed by describing the family as 'the domestic church'[38]. But the phrase is a heavy one and may not convey the meaning. It can even make for a gap between family and church. 'Church' can suggest structure and institution rather than activities; or it can suggest activities that are out of the ordinary run of life. But here we are thinking of church, or parish as people – as a community of Christians, engaged in the kind of activities that are characteristic of the Gospel.

It might be clearer if we describe the family instead as 'the basic Christian community'. That phrase is usually used to refer, especially in the Southern Hemisphere, to small groups of Christians who gather regularly to pray and share around Gospel and life. Here I am adding another meaning to this – that the most basic community of Christians is the family. This is because it is the basic place where the activities that are the heart of the Gospel are going on.

Sacramental

You may say that church/parish is more than these activities. In particular, you might want to say that the sacraments are a big part of what goes on in the parish. That is true, but there is a link here also. I am thinking of the parallel between the parish community gathering for Eucharist and the family gathering for dinner.

Part of the parallel is that both fall short! In too many cases, the parish 'under-performs' when it comes to Eucharist. The turn-out may be disappointing. What goes on can be pedestrian, routine, lifeless, dispiriting. It is the same with families. They can neglect to gather. Their meals can be functional, rushed, lacking in family spirit.

But at their best, family and parish are very similar too. The family meal can be a sharing of lives as well as of food, shot through with remembering, with happiness, a time of bonding and a time of refreshing. The Eucharist can be filled with togetherness and prayer, also remembering, also nourishing. So, already at the family table, there is something Eucharistic, something sacramental. And there is something of a real presence.

A parallel can be seen with the Sacrament of Reconciliation too, even if it has fallen on hard times in today's church. The elements that make up its celebration are traditionally called contrition, confession, satisfaction and absolution. It is striking that it is the same dynamic going on in family life – failing and feeling sorry, apologising and being forgiven, reconciling and making good.

In the conflicts and interactions within a family, people can discover God's true face as forgiveness. If this is the case, then again there is something sacramental going on, a kind of anticipation of what is going on in the larger family we call church. With both sacraments, Eucharist and Reconciliation, we can see how 'church' is already happening in the family's activities of table fellowship and reconciliation. There is something of sacramental grace in family life.

Affirmation
All this brings up again a theme already highlighted, that of affirmation. Church and family are intimately linked. What goes on in family life is at the heart of what Christian community is all about. This invites the larger Christian community of the parish to develop a 'ministry of affirmation' to the smaller Christian community of the family.

I recall someone speaking once about canonisation, the thousands and thousands of people over the centuries who have been declared saints by the church. He asked the group; how many can you think of who were mothers or fathers? There was much silence and very few answers – lots of popes and bishops, lots of virgins and martyrs, but hardly any mothers or fathers!

This reflects a huge failure of affirmation. Lots of people, as they bring up their families, are living with huge generosity, courage and commitment, amidst various struggles and adversities, keeping hope alive as best they can. Increasingly they are not churchgoers, though many pray. They are generally not 'involved' in the parish.

And yet: 'involved' is about much more than parish ministries and parish groups. 'Involved' firstly means living the Christian way in the ordinary circumstances of daily life. If this is so, then the *most* involved in the parish are mostly unseen, mostly mothers and fathers. It is just that they may not see the link and so their 'involvement' is below awareness-level and below recognition-level.

The ministry of affirmation is about making the link. When people see that what is going on in their families is *already* 'church' – when they are affirmed in this way – then they can come to feel involved. They can feel validated in their faith, in their spiritual lives. Such affirmation can be the start of a new trajectory in their spiritual journey.

I have often recounted the story a friend of mine tells about the birth of her first child; all the expectation and apprehension; all her energy focused on the child and on everything going well. All did go well and the day after the birth she was able to go to Mass in the hospital oratory.

The words of consecration were like an explosion in her head. 'This is my body, given up for you... This is my blood, poured out for you.' She exclaimed to herself; 'Jesus, I know what you mean!' It is a dramatic instance of someone making the link – the self-giving at the heart of the Gospel and the self-giving at the heart of the family. In less dramatic ways, but no less real, it is a link that is waiting to be made in so many families.

'Family' – a Word for Church

Second, what might it mean to say that 'family' is a word for church, an image for what Christian community is meant to be? We move here from the parish being called to evangelise, to the parish itself being evangelised. On the one hand, the parish's 'ministry of affirmation' proclaims to the family the good news of what family is. Now, on the other hand, the parish opens itself to be inspired and evangelised, by the lives of families, into its own inner reality.

The link is already there in the chapter about the parish. I quoted John Paul II's picture of the parish as 'the family of God...

a familial and welcoming home'. He draws on the language of home and family to talk about the parish. It is a language that the Christian community can take to itself – a quite appropriate language with which to depict itself and articulate what it is called to be. It is activities language – he also says that the parish, like the family, is not principally a structure or an institution.

So we have a mutual interaction. The parish seeks to reveal the family to itself, affirming how in its basic activities it is already being church, the basic Christian community, the Lord truly present. But in this, the family is at the same time revealing the larger Christian community to itself – inviting, calling, challenging it to be family and to be a family of families.

The challenge is real. To speak of church and parish as 'home' is obviously attractive. But church has not always been an experience of home for people and has often been quite the opposite. (This has been true of families also.) 'Home' is welcoming, inclusive; but many have felt unwelcome, excluded, judged. Church even today can look like an exclusive club with rigorous rules defining membership.

This tension offers a different perspective on Luke's parable of the prodigal son. Usually, and rightly, the parable is taken as an imaging of God. But it can also be taken as an imaging of church. This is especially appropriate when we realise that church is itself meant to be an image of God, a portrayal of God, in how it comports itself.

As the prodigal returns, the father stands for the God of Jesus Christ, welcoming, embracing. The other son stands for something less generous, begrudging, judgmental, however understandable his feelings. These in turn are two images for church, parish, Christian community – one that is a welcoming home, the other more like an exclusive club.

The family reveals the parish to itself because, in seeking to be the best it can be, it is revealing God to the larger Christian family

– the God of Jesus Christ as portrayed in the parable of the prodigal son. When the parish is not in touch with itself as family, as home – when it falls short of itself – it may be the families in the parish that are most alive to what is wrong.

Sunday – and Beyond

Perhaps it is Sunday when the challenge is most real. The families in the parish call on the larger community to put care into its weekly gatherings. Gathering for Eucharist is meant to be imbued with a sense of family. It is meant to have a strong sense of welcome, of occasion, of coming together for something special, of being a special group of people. This reinforces what was said in the chapter on praying, about the 'horizontal' dimension of the Eucharist.

Is there any other single thing that would transform our experience of Eucharist as much as this? Parishes that have attended to this can confirm the point. When Eucharist reflects family meals at their best – the togetherness, the belonging, the intimacy and depth – then the worshipping community is in touch with itself and experiencing what it is to be church.

When we are then sent from the Lord's Table, the challenge ripples out. Those who gather may feel 'at home', feel the warmth of Christian family and belonging. But sending points us to those who are not present. There are certainly people out there who do not feel that they belong or who would not feel at home. The chapter on welcome reflected on who they might be.

'Home' was famously described by Robert Frost (in his poem, 'The Death of the Hired Man') – 'the place where, when you have to go there, They have to take you in… Something you somehow haven't to deserve'. Even for the 'black sheep', there is usually a place at the table! After all, they are 'family'. We are 'sent' in that spirit, challenging ourselves with the question; how can we, in what we do and how we are, send out the message that we are all family?

Concentric

It is like concentric circles – a smaller circle representing the family; a bigger circle representing the parish, the larger Christian family, the family of families. Both have the same centre, the core that is the Gospel, with the activities that characterise the Gospel, activities distinctive of the God of Jesus. These activities are the centre of each circle, the heart of family and the heart of parish.

Parish and family are united on concentric paths of transformation. They each have their struggles – some similar, some different – but they are called in the same direction. They are each called to live more and more out of that Gospel core. Along the path, each mirrors the other, each calls and affirms and challenges the other.

An expression of this is found in John Paul II's message on the family. There he says that the partners' love is 'the permanent reminder to the church of what happened on the cross[39].' At first this may sound off-putting but in fact it goes to the heart of what unites family and parish.

What happened on the cross was not mainly a gruesome execution. And John Paul's phrase is certainly not meant to convey that family life is a crucifixion! What happened on the cross was indescribable self-giving. Brendan Kennelly wrote a poem ('A Giving') about the God who is 'determined to hold on to nothing', who 'gives everything away... such constant evacuation of the heart, such striving towards emptiness'. This is what we see revealed in Jesus' self-giving on the cross.

There is hardly a closer comparison to this self-giving than that of parents – first in giving birth (as with the woman I spoke of), then in the ongoing other-centredness of bringing up a family, the daily grind of going beyond self, the staying generous even in adversity, the finding one's happiness in the happiness of another. Such family life is the 'permanent reminder' in the parish, and to the parish, of what parish is all about.

We come back to the consecration at Mass, the divine 'striving towards emptiness'. I wonder how many parents see themselves in this moment, this action? Our conditioning has led us to look on rather than to enter in. But we are meant to enter in. Parents are meant to see that their self-giving is intimately bound up with this self-giving of Jesus, the self-giving of God.

It is not just parents. All who gather are to see themselves in the consecration, to see themselves 'in God'. In this moment, families remind the whole gathering what their existence is all about. In this moment, the church proclaims to families their own inner mystery.

A Suggestion

These reflections argue for a deep connection between family and parish, in their shared journey into the mystery of the Gospel. The connection is being made stronger through the life-giving initiatives in today's parish. At the same time, these reflections suggest that it would be worth giving even more attention to the link.

It might be worth having a group in the parish focused on all this alone, a kind of 'family affirmation group'. It would have a single task, to build up consciousness of the link between family and parish – to explore ways in which families can be affirmed as church, and to explore how to develop the parish's consciousness of itself as family.

An example is the suggestion in the chapter on caring. It could develop a network of contact people around the parish; people who would become attentive to the families in their locality and who would meet to pray and to share what they have become aware of. Out of that exercise, practical ways would emerge of showing families that they are noticed and of saying to them, 'we care that you exist'.

Such a group would in fact be imitating Jesus, imitating his activity of noticing and caring for families. Think of his healing visit to the house of Peter and his ill mother-in-law (Mark 1); of his visit to the home of Jairus and his dying daughter (Mark 5); of his visits to the house of Martha and Mary, including at the death of their brother Lazarus (Luke 10; John 11); of his compassion for the widow of Nain at the death of her son (Luke 7); of his attention to the father whose son was epileptic (Luke 9). As the parish group attends to families in the spirit of Jesus, people will feel noticed and affirmed, faith and hope will grow.

The group could also have a role in affirming other parish groups in their ministry to families – funeral and bereavement ministry; Baptism, Communion and Confirmation ministry; family Mass; initiatives for engaged couples; initiatives marking wedding anniversaries. An occasion bringing such ministries together could deepen the parish's sense of family, perhaps throwing up new approaches or initiatives.

'Holy'
A final thought on the 'holy' family of Nazareth, Mary, Joseph and Jesus. Why do we call it holy? Is it because it is so different from 'ordinary' families? Yes and no. 'Yes' in the sense that this is the Incarnation come about, therefore a unique place and a unique family.

But also 'no'. For this family from Nazareth is a symbol of hope for every family. They did not fit the normal structure of 'family'. Their circumstances were not the 'normal' ones. There is plenty of evidence of struggle and of anxiety – having to flee from home; the twelve-year-old going missing; coping with the strange unfolding drama of his later years and premature death.

So it is also a very ordinary family. This is where divine presence is found – in real life, in the adversity as much as the contentment, in the daily discovery of generous spirit. This is holiness; this is Gospel; this is what Christian community is about.

SECTION D

Organising Ourselves

CHAPTER FIFTEEN
Getting People Involved

We began by reflecting on *where* we are, the situation of today's parish. Then we turned to *what* we are, rediscovering a deep sense of our identity as a faith community. We went on to explore *how* tomorrow's parish can express itself as an evangelising parish. This leads us, finally, to the *who*, the people in the faith community, and how they organise or mobilise themselves in their mission.

Everyone will be aware of the challenges here. For quite a while now, the cry in every parish has been about how hard it is to get people involved. On top of that, both priests and congregations are ageing. There are fewer and fewer priests. It is hard to see who the 'who' is going to be. This makes the topic of the present chapter crucial.

There is no magical answer, and it is going to be a long-term process. But there is a way forward. In what follows I will be arguing that the main issue is how we see what the issue is! When that has been teased out, there will be some specific suggestions about 'getting people involved'.

FEELING INVOLVED

I think the place to start is with the word 'involvement'. I would propose a fundamental distinction between people 'getting involved' and people 'feeling involved'. In many ways this is the key to the whole question. Helping people to feel involved is primary.

A simple reflection on Sunday Eucharist gives us a way into it. There is the priest. There may be a choir. There are ministers of the Word and ministers of the Eucharist. There are the servers, ushers perhaps, the collectors. And there is the congregation. Out of all those people, who would we say is 'involved'?

We might be inclined to say that those who are doing more things are more involved. But that is not necessarily the case. After all, people's minds can be a hundred miles away from what they are doing. The person who is most involved might well be somebody sitting down the church, 'doing' nothing. But that person may be participating intensely; listening to the Scripture, bringing their concerns to the altar, feeling at home, going away refreshed and challenged.

What matters most is that people *feel* involved. If people feel involved, then they *are* involved, often in a very profound way. The main issue is not about getting people involved in specific parish activities. Of course that is important, but it is a narrower idea, and a short-term way of looking at things. The main issue is about feeling involved.

This follows on from all that has preceded. The parish has been envisaged as a ministering community. As someone once put it, it is not a 'parish of ministries' but a 'ministering parish'. A parish of ministries is one where some people are involved in specific groups or projects. Even if there were a lot of them, it would still be only a few, only a small percentage of the faith community. But a ministering parish is one where everybody is involved. They are not, by and large, in ministry groups. But they feel involved.

A ministering parish community is a place of every member ministry. It is a place where Baptism is not lying dormant, or in sleep mode, as it were. Baptism is not a thing of the past. This is a parish where people have activated their Baptism and are engaging with it. It is a place where people are in touch with their faith, in the heart, in the head, in the hands. None of that necessarily requires 'getting involved' in a parish ministry. But it does mean feeling involved. It is a different sense of involvement.

A Common Thread
This links back to the chapters of the last section. We described how the evangelising parish expresses itself in caring, in welcoming, in listening and in praying. Now we can see how the theme of feeling involved is implicit in each of these. When the parish expresses itself in these ways – when these come to the fore in the parish – it has the effect of more people coming to feel involved.

The chapter on caring, as well as that on family, highlighted the ministry of affirmation. We talked of how so many people live caring lives. Affirmation does not ask them to do anything more. It names what is *already* going on and recognises it as 'being involved'. All it asks of people is that they recognise it too, that they make the link between this and their Baptism, so as to see how this is 'faith in the hands'.

Those chapters went on to highlight how the faith community can become more aware, in order to notice the needs in people's lives. This was a theme in the chapter on listening also. When we notice, then we can respond. If people feel noticed and cared for, that can be a form of feeling involved. They can come to feel that they belong.

The chapter on welcome referred to different life-giving initiatives in the parish in recent times. It seems fair to say that the secret of success has been the welcome that people experience.

People have felt accepted and appreciated. They have come to feel that they belong. Again, many have come to feel involved, to feel a part of the faith community.

The chapter also outlined some challenges around welcome. There are many who, for different reasons, do not feel 'inside', who may feel unwelcome. They too can come to feel involved. They can be noticed. They can come to feel accepted as they are, whatever their story. If they come to feel that the parish is 'home', with a place for them at the table, they are coming to feel involved.

In the chapter on listening, we spoke about the people within the faith community having a voice, having their experience and wisdom valued. We also spoke about the parish listening to people 'out there', to learn from their spirituality. Listening like this is dignifying. It gives people a sense of being respected and appreciated. Again, it can make people feel involved, or more involved than they already felt.

Finally, in the chapter on praying, we talked about the possibilities for connecting with people's lives and faith through different prayer occasions. In this, people feel noticed, feel welcome, feel cared for. The connection helps people, who may have felt on the outside, to feel involved. Again, many of the ideas about enhancing the experience of Eucharist are about deepening the feeling of being involved.

None of this is about 'getting people involved'. It is about something more fundamental, something foundational. It about creating an environment of inclusion, where people feel faith connecting with life, where people have a sense of ministering and being ministered to, where people feel that they are 'practising' their faith.

The aim here is that everyone would feel involved. But that is not measurable in the way that aiming for a full church is. If more people feel involved, that would be reflected to some extent in attendances. But not everybody will come to church regularly.

Not everybody will identify openly with parish. When the faith community is caring, welcoming, listening and praying with people, there will always be more people than we know who are feeling a part of it, feeling involved.

GETTING INVOLVED

Feeling involved is foundational, the overarching focus. Getting people involved in specific parish ministries and initiatives is more specific, and secondary. But here, at the same time, we need to review our understanding, our ideas about what is involved in getting people involved.

Some say that it is next to impossible to get people involved in the parish, or that people no longer want to be involved. But others say that people are willing, that it is just a matter of how to connect with them. Both views are valid, but I am inclined to think that the latter view may be nearer the truth. Getting people involved is difficult, but possible.

Obstacles

A good place to begin is by asking about the obstacles. What is it that prevents people from getting involved in specific parish activities? When we think about it, it becomes clear that there is no single answer. There are quite a number of different factors at play.

Some people do not want to get involved. They do not see beyond availing of the services. Or they go along when it suits them. This is part of something broader, the conditioning of generations. In a clerical church, people do not get involved. Apart from helping out here and there, people are recipients of ministry. Participation, ownership, co-responsibility are not part of the mindset. It takes a long time to break down that culture.

Another factor is peer pressure. It arises out of this culture.

People can be put off getting involved by the reaction of peers. They find others calling them a 'holy Joe' or that kind of thing. Or they can be put off by family members. Or they can be put off by the reaction of fellow parishioners, people whose attitude seems to be, 'who does he think he is?' or 'soon she'll want to be running the parish'.

Again, there are people who find that their lives are too full or too pressured to allow for any specific involvement, often parents with young families. Maybe they would consider it at another time, but now is not the right time. What is needed here is not pressure to get involved, but affirmation of how they are already deeply involved.

There are also people who are open to getting involved, but are frightened off by what they see. It is the 'same old faces', year after year. It can look like a life sentence! Also, some feel that they may not be treated as equals. Maybe it is still a clerical-style parish, where getting involved means helping the priest. There can also be a 'hierarchy' among parish volunteers, where some regard themselves as superior and more important.

Then there are people who find that their parish is not inviting. It is not personal enough, it lacks warmth. Some may have had a bad experience that put them off. Part of it is that parish groups can appear uninviting. They can look like a clique or a closed shop, where newcomers are not welcome.

A big factor is that quite a lot of people simply lack confidence. They would love to contribute, but they feel that they have nothing to offer. They may feel inferior. They may think that they lack the knowledge or skills required. Or they may just not believe in themselves. These people are never going to just come forward. They will need encouragement and affirmation before anything happens.

Linked to this, there are many people who would have become involved long ago, except that nobody ever asked them! Here, asking is more than an announcement in church or in a newsletter. It is one person inviting another. There are lots of people who will not put themselves forward. They need to be asked, personally, individually. Many are waiting to be asked.

A clearer picture is emerging. There is no one reason to explain why it is hard to get people involved. There are different factors. There is the conditioning of generations, and the attendant peer pressure. There is time pressure. There is lack of confidence. There are the ways parish itself puts people off.

At the same time, there is much openness and willingness that remains untapped. What comes across overall is that there are more possibilities than perhaps we appreciate. There is much that is possible. Once we appreciate the obstacles that are there, we can start to see ways of addressing them. I will now outline four parts of a possible approach.

Think 'Everybody'

First, the long-term goal is every member ministry, a ministering community. We have to keep this in mind. If we only look at the short term, at 'getting people involved', at filling gaps, then we will only find short-term outcomes. The underlying problems will continue unresolved.

So, all that has been said about being welcoming and affirming applies here. Every member ministry is an end in itself. It is the basic form of 'involvement'. Young families, parents busy bringing up young children, are the primary example of this. At the same time, if there is a growing sense of being a ministering community, it will have the by-product that more people will be willing to take on specific involvements.

The way we participate in Eucharist is relevant here. There may be hundreds of people in church. Yet there may be no minister of the Word. There may be just one or two ministers of the Eucharist. There may be hardly anybody joining in the singing (if there is singing). The theory is that we are celebrating the Eucharist together. But it is more like the priest saying Mass for us. This could be a good place to start.

There is no reason why most people in the church could not be ministers of the Eucharist. Nearly everyone can sing. Everybody can say the responses. A lot of people could read. But we demand so little of ourselves. We need to expect more of ourselves. The way we celebrate the Eucharist sends out a message about what we aspire to be as a parish. If we aim to maximise Eucharistic participation, the sense of co-celebration, we are setting a standard for ourselves – the standard of every member ministry.

Make Ministry Attractive
Second, there are things we can do to make ministry attractive. For one thing, we can 'reform' the habits of parish groups. A parish group cannot be a closed shop. It cannot be a life sentence. Regular turnover of membership should be the norm. Often now this is the case with parish pastoral councils. That is a model to follow. People should not be pressurised to stay on. It should be clear – and adhered to – that involvement is fixed-term.

Related to this, people are more inclined to get involved if the involvement looks real and manageable. It is not attractive if the 'job description' is vague. Involvement is not attractive if it has no limits. It is different if there is a clear task, a clearly worthwhile aim, and parameters on the commitment. For instance, if I am told that it will last four months, that it requires one hour a week, and that it will produce such-and-such an outcome, I am already more disposed to saying yes.

Again, when people's involvement is sought today, they want to know 'what's in it for me?' It is not a selfish question. It is fair to ask. Sometimes what comes across in the parish is that a small, ageing, beleaguered, struggling group of people are looking for others to share in their agony. The message needs to be appealing, about a joy rather than a chore.

Ministry is both a giving and a receiving. Those involved want to give something; they want to make a difference. But they also enjoy the involvement and feel enriched. Often they say that they receive more than they give. Giving is good for people, and doing something for others is also good for ourselves. When we ask people to get involved, we can put this positive message across.

See Ministries Differently

Third, to generate specific involvements, we could do with seeing parish ministries in a slightly different way. As a mental exercise, compose two lists. One of them is a list of ministries that currently operate in the parish. So, for instance, you might write down ministers of the Eucharist, the parish bulletin, the Baptism team, or those running the parish finances.

The other is a list of needs. Think back to the chapters on care and welcome, listening and prayer. Each of those reflections brought up many needs and many possibilities. The very themes themselves are at the heart of what parish is. They create awareness. They point us to what we may not have been thinking of. They look beyond the perspective of what we are already doing.

The existing ministries are not exhaustive. They do not cover everything. There are gaps. If we think of ourselves as an evangelising parish, we think of themes like care, welcome, listening, prayer. That in turn shapes how we see parish ministries and what ministries are needed. If we start with existing ministries, we may see no further. However, if we start with the themes, we are letting the needs call forth the ministries that are 'not yet'.

So, if we want to get people involved, we could ask; involved in what? It could be existing ministries. Or it could be *new* ministries, in response to needs that are not currently being addressed. The evangelising parish focuses on the latter, without neglecting the former. This may well have the effect of reaching more people. It can reach people who might be more attracted to a new initiative than to joining an existing group.

Make Contact
The fourth part of a possible approach concerns how we make contact with people. A notice at Mass or in a newsletter may be useful for not excluding anyone, but there is rarely much response. Personal contact is the single most effective way of involving people in parish ministries. There are many people, with great gifts and some time on their hands, who would respond gladly if there were a personal contact. Personal contact can make someone feel wanted. It can reassure them about the contribution they could make.

Priests obviously have a huge role here because they have come in contact with so many people through their ministry. But other people have an even bigger role. The priest can encourage people to see that they have every right to invite fellow parishioners to become involved. This is every member ministry. Everybody knows somebody who would enjoy being involved. Everyone knows someone who has something to offer. All they need is for a friend or neighbour to say, 'I think you would be great at that.'

Finally, parishes have had success with 'ministry days'. For instance, there could be a big display in the parish hall, where different groups have their own stalls with their work presented for everyone to come and admire. This would be supported by homilies, together with a good quality brochure and reply forms. Ideally it would also include some space for publicising some new initiatives being proposed to the parish.

THE DIRECT FOCUS

This chapter may represent something of a sea change in how we see and approach the challenge of getting people involved. We have a tendency to concentrate on existing ministries. We tend to think in terms of how we can recruit people for these ministries. It is a valid concern, but if it is the main focus, it misses the point.

Our concentration, firstly, has to be on every member ministry. Then the focus is broader, on more than just maintaining existing ministries. It is on every person feeling the sense of welcome and belonging, feeling affirmed, feeling involved. It is on a ministering parish rather than a parish of ministries. As well, our concentration has to be on needs rather than just on existing ministries. Thinking in terms of care, of welcome, of listening, of prayer can bring the needs of the parish to light.

The two go together, as a kind of twin focus. On the one hand there is a growing awareness of the real needs that make a call on the faith community. On the other, there is a growing culture of every member ministry. If we bring the two into sharper focus, and if we become more conscious of them, they can then become the focus of our efforts.

CHAPTER SIXTEEN
Parish Ministry Groups

The evangelising parish expresses itself through all its members, through every member ministry. And it expresses itself through the various parish ministries and ministry groups, each with its own specific focus. This chapter is about all these ministries becoming cohesive elements in the parish's pursuit of its aim. This will involve discussing their needs, especially the need to build their spirituality and unite them in a shared vision.

PARISH MINISTRIES TODAY

Each group involved in parish ministry has its own experience. The concerns of ministers of the Eucharist are not the same as those of a youth ministry group. A choir and a communications group have different questions and concerns. But, alongside this variety, there are some common positives and negatives in their experience.

Positives
On the positive side is the great enrichment these ministries bring to parish life. Imagine parish liturgy without the different ministries, including those behind the scenes. Think of how care groups, visitation groups, bereavement groups and hospitality

groups have deepened the experience of welcome and belonging in the community. Think of how Baptism and funeral teams, First Communion and Confirmation teams create such effective outreach to people 'on the fringes'. Think of how finance committees and building committees have helped give a new injection of life in many parishes.

Also on the positive side is what the experience has meant for the people in these groups. For many it has meant a new and exciting experience of church. It has meant a new sense of vocation for both priests and people, as they work together, sharing their gifts, in ministry groups and pastoral councils. Many have come to a deeper and richer faith through their involvement.

Concerns

There are also concerns that need to be articulated. Some of these came up in the last chapter. The issue of recruitment looms large, with the refrain of the 'same old faces'. When it was teased out, it became clear that one part of the problem lay with the ministry groups themselves.

The success of a group can also be its undoing. Some groups become very close-knit and can appear exclusive, even if not intending to be. Another aspect is that parish groups do not usually have a system of rollover membership in place. People end up being there for years on end. Maybe they feel pressurised, or maybe it is their own doing.

Another concern is that, in some ministries, the work becomes more of a job or a routine than a ministry. This may be more true of ministries that do not have a strong group aspect to them. For instance, ministers of the Word and ministers of the Eucharist are vulnerable to this. They are not so much a group as a collection of individuals. Once they are trained in, they may be left to themselves. It can become just a slot on a rota.

But it is broader than this. By and large, parish groups do not attend to themselves. They do not take care of their members' needs. They give generously of themselves and their time, but they neglect to give time to themselves. The well may run dry. The spirituality that supports and carries their ministry can weaken. The inspiration can evaporate.

Again, it is a concern that parish ministry groups usually are disconnected. Each group is taking care of its own task and may be doing so very well. But there tends to be little or no communication or coordination between groups. People may have little idea what goes on in other groups and what they are doing. It all tends to be compartmentalised. All are parts of a jigsaw, except that there is no jigsaw, no complete picture, only the individual pieces. And instead of coordination and cooperation, there can even be rivalry and territoriality.

Finally, there is a concern that was voiced in the last chapter. The parish may have a great variety of flourishing ministry groups. It can be easy to conclude that, because there is so much going on, all that needs to be done is being done. But rarely, if ever, is there such a neat match between what is being done and what needs to be done. There are real needs that our very success may prevent us from seeing.

Spirituality and Renewal
Going back to groups not taking care of themselves, I want to draw on Pope Francis' *The Joy of the Gospel*, where he reflects at length (fifteen pages) on 'Temptations faced by Pastoral Workers' (he includes priests in this).[40] A lot of what he says relates to people involved in parish ministries and is very relevant here. I will list a number of the observations he makes.

He speaks of a 'cooling of fervour', where the work becomes 'a mere appendage to their life, as if it were not part of their very identity'. He also notes the temptation 'to avoid any responsibility that may take away from their free time ... Some resist giving themselves over completely to mission and thus end up in a state of paralysis.'

He talks of an 'inferiority complex', brought on by a 'scepticism with regard to the church's message' in today's culture; so that people 'conceal their Christian identity and convictions'. They end up 'being unhappy' and 'stifling the joy of mission'. He also notes 'a defeatism which turns us into querulous and disillusioned pessimists, "sourpusses". Nobody can go off to battle unless he is fully convinced of victory beforehand.'

He talks about 'activity undertaken badly, without adequate motivation, without a spirituality that would permeate it and make it pleasurable. As a result, work becomes more tiring than necessary.' He goes on to talk about a 'melancholy' that 'seizes the heart' so that people are 'robbed of the joy of evangelisation'.

He talks of 'the vainglory of those who are content to have a modicum of power and would rather be the general of a defeated army than a mere private in a unit which continues to fight'. Not unrelated to this, he notes 'envy and jealousy, even among Christians ... a spirit of exclusivity, creating an "inner circle" ... this or that group which thinks itself different or special.'

He speaks of people who are 'tied to tasks within the church, without a real commitment to applying the Gospel to the transformation of society'. He speaks of 'an ostentatious preoccupation for the liturgy, for doctrine and for the church's prestige, but without any concern that the Gospel has a real impact on God's faithful people in the concrete needs of the present time'.

For anybody involved in ministry, it adds up to quite an examination of conscience! Some of what Francis observes brings to mind the question 'whose needs are being served here?' Most of all, what he says points to the vital need for spirituality. There needs to be ongoing attention to the spiritual renewal of all those who minister.

The Purpose of Parish Ministries

An important part of the spirituality is a shared sense of purpose. Here I want to return to the point about parish groups being disconnected, and to reflect on the fundamental purpose of these groups.

Underlying the specific purposes of different groups is a common aim that in fact is the heart of each group's work. Generally speaking, this aim is dormant in the consciousness of groups themselves, as their attention is absorbed by the task in hand. Or is 'dormant' too kind? Maybe there never has been a shared sense of purpose, an aim held in common.

Here we may recall the story of the cathedral from chapter six, together with that chapter's articulation of a vision of parish. People in parish ministry need to articulate the shared purpose of all the groups and ministries. This is essential for breaking down the compartmentalisation and building cohesion instead, the cohesiveness of an evangelising parish.

Vision and Cohesion

In the diagrams below, each 'ministry' stands for a different parish ministry or ministry group. The first diagram represents

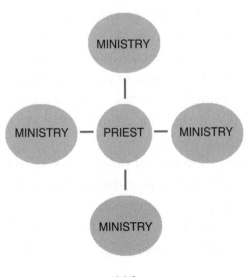

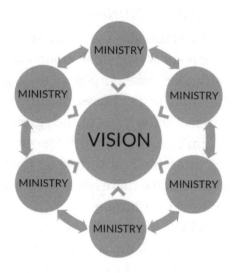

one kind of parish, more yesterday's than today's. The different ministries do their separate things. They are not linked one to another. The only common denominator is the priest. Indeed, the people in these groups may see themselves as 'helping the priest', assisting him with *his* ministry.

The second diagram stands for tomorrow's parish. There is still a priest, a leader, but ministry is no longer centred on him. The centre now is the vision. All the ministries and ministry groups find their unity in the vision of the parish they aspire to. Instead of the previous compartmentalisation, they each see themselves as part of a jigsaw – because now there is a complete jigsaw, and a sense of what it might look like. They see the different things they are doing, not as discrete activities, but as components that add up to something greater.

As regards the vision itself, I propose seeing it here in terms of every member ministry. The parish we aspire to – the vision inspiring each ministry group – is a ministering community, where each member *feels* involved. This is one way of stating the aim of each and every parish ministry. The 'surface' aim of each is to complete their specific task. But, in completing their task, the underlying aim of each is to enable or activate the ministry of all God's people.

Each group is there to serve. But service is more than providing a service. Rather, service means being at the service of Baptism's call. The work of the groups is done, not when a task has been completed, or a service provided. The work is done when God's people are experiencing themselves as a ministering community.

An Enabling Style of Ministry

A good practical illustration of what is meant by an enabling style of ministry comes from the parish's music ministry. Many choirs see themselves in a performing role. A lot of their fulfilment comes through challenging themselves to ever higher quality. Yet today's goal of a ministering community hinges on participation. It asks that we maximise the singing of the congregation. This is no small challenge, seeing how conditioned people are to being passive at Mass.

Obviously a balance is the ideal, a balance of performance and participation. Thus the ministry of the cantor has been developing. He or she is in front of us, not to perform, but to facilitate our performance, our singing. His or her aim is to enable the participation of all, to activate every member ministry.

In a similar way, each parish group needs to articulate how its particular ministry is at the service of the ministry of all. Think of the people who clean and decorate the church. That certainly seems to be just a job. But if, when people come to the church, they feel the warmth of the ambience, they also feel welcome. They feel at home, they feel they belong. The ministry helps them to feel involved.

Think of the ministers of the Word. They are not just 'doing the reading'. Think of the phrase, 'only say the word and I shall be healed'. The reading is an event; the Word does something. The idea is that a link is made in the listeners' hearts between the Word and their lives. If that happens, discipleship is deepened. People have a new sense of their own ministry.

Think of the Baptism team. They do more than just go through the practicalities of the ceremony with the parents. They make the occasion an experience of welcome. And if they also involve the worshipping community welcoming the families, then they are also facilitating the community in taking ownership of its ministry of welcome. Thus both the family and the community are brought to a new level of engagement.

Think of the ministers of the Eucharist. When they say 'the body of Christ', they are not making an announcement or repeating a formula. They are telling us who we are. They are saying, 'when you receive the body of Christ, you become the body of Christ'. That is what we are meant to experience at each Eucharist. Every member ministry means feeling like a member of the body of Christ.

And, in aiming to facilitate every member ministry, people in parish groups have a witnessing role. They are not just 'helping Father'. The ministry they exercise is *theirs*. They are expressing their Baptism, giving shape to their vocation. And this is witness. It is like holding up a mirror to people, allowing them to see a reflection of their own Baptism. In this way, others can be encouraged in their call to every member ministry.

SUPPORTING PARISH GROUPS

In this context we can look at some of the ways in which parish groups can be supported in their shared aim. The parish pastoral council has the key part to play, for such support is a part of its distinctive role.

Encouragement

It is very important for the parish leadership to pay attention, to acknowledge, to appreciate, to affirm. To this end, the pastoral council has to create a relationship with all the groups in the parish. For example, there could be some kind of liaison system, where different members of the council connect with different groups. While respectful of each group's autonomy, they would express interest. They would invite feedback. They would offer practical support.

This might be a stepping stone to further ways of encouraging parish groups. For instance, the council might look for ways to communicate with the parish about all that is being done by the groups. Here I am thinking of the good that can be done simply by proclaiming all that is going on in the parish. In most parishes people do not realise the half of it. When they do they can be enormously appreciative.

One parish took up the image of the vine and the branches. Along one wall of the church they arranged a long (artificial) vine, the branches decorated with large print descriptions and photos of the different parish groups, and the parish vision statement at the centre. Besides being a revelation to parishioners, it was a big encouragement to people in the various groups.

The parish can also celebrate the voluntary. Many parishes host a social event as a way of thanking all the people involved. Sometimes this includes a liturgical element, a celebration of the Eucharist or a creative ritual. That prayer element provides a context for expressing something of the meaning of the different ministries. People can be deeply affirmed in the spiritual meaning and value of what they do.

Enrichment

The experience of ministry is itself meant to be enriching, but this needs to be complemented by providing enrichment in more specific ways. Many groups begin their life with some form of training or initiation. This can be quite formative. But after that it is down to work. Further opportunities for refreshment and renewal can be rare. When the group meets, conversations tend to go no further than the task in hand.

Enrichment sessions could focus on generating a renewed sense of the group's role. This can help groups appreciate the deeper significance of their work. They can come to see how, in and through their own specific role, they are also helping to bring a truly ministering community into being. It can also help them deepen the spirituality that they bring to their work. The vision that emerges can inspire and energise the group.

Enrichment can also have elements of evaluation and re-training. It is an opportunity to weed out bad practices and to name good practice. It is an opportunity too to look at how the organisation of this particular ministry could be made more effective. In all of this the group is learning a more proactive ownership of its ministry.

Networking

This idea picks up again on compartmentalisation, where there is little interaction or integration between the parish ministries, and a lack of overall cohesion in the work of the parish as a whole. Networking can address this situation.

Meeting together in clusters can be a springboard for collaboration. For instance, there may be a few groups who are in the general area of caring ministries. There are others who are all involved in music ministry. Such sets of groups can share their experience of ministry. They can streamline their operation.

Communication will help to overcome any jealousies there are. Hopefully any sense of territoriality will be dissipated.

Ultimately, networking can lead to common vision. Groups can be brought into an inspiring sense of the vision of parish that they all share. An assembly of all parish groups could be very valuable here. And, as the parish enters into a planning mode, each group can see how its effort fits into an overall scheme, like the parts of the body in St Paul's image, each of them vital in its own distinctive way.

Recruiting

Perhaps the first need that most groups will express is that of getting new members. In this area the pastoral council can offer both a support and a challenge.

On the support side, the council could organise a parish day as mentioned above, or a 'Ministering Sunday' where there is an invitation from the altar to join specified groups. At the same time, groups can be reminded that personal one-to-one contact remains the most effective way of recruiting.

On the challenge side, groups need to ensure that they are welcoming and open to newcomers. Being welcoming also means having a rollover of membership. This would also include a change of the group coordinator every few years. It should be almost a principle that people have to move on.

The Actual Needs

Going back to an earlier point, there is a further challenge that is addressed to the pastoral council rather than to any particular ministry group. The council needs to look beyond all that is currently being done. It needs to ascertain what needs are not being attended to. It needs to look beyond the groups that are in existence, and to think about the groups that have yet to be.

To do this effectively it has to engage in a wide consultation. The people who are already involved have a certain perspective. They are often older; they are usually churchgoers; they tend to be relatively content and secure. Broader listening is needed, with more people involved in unearthing or articulating needs. Within such a process, people might also be more inclined to become involved in addressing the needs they themselves have helped to identify.

COMMITMENT TO QUALITY

Perhaps what comes out most strongly from this chapter is the need to invest more in building up the parish groups themselves. People need ongoing formation. There needs to be a move away from seeing involvement as a job or task and towards seeing it as a ministry. It will make a big difference if people involved in parish groups develop the spirituality that inspires and drives their ministry.

It will also make a big difference if people develop a vision around their ministry. They can be helped to see beyond the specific task they are engaged in. They need to come to a sense of what it is that all the different parish ministries are feeding into. In particular, their work will be transformed if it is inspired by the vision of every member ministry. They will come to see themselves as parts of the jigsaw, working together as an evangelising parish.

Parish ministries are meant to be both voluntary and professional. The voluntary spirit will always be central. But it has to be accompanied by a commitment to quality. That is what the word 'professional' means here. It is interesting that the word has a religious connotation, such as when we speak of religious profession. In that sense, 'professional' ministry is imbued with commitment. It is inspired by the commitment of Baptism. It is committed to our vision of parish. And it is committed to achieving the highest standards in realising that vision.

CHAPTER SEVENTEEN
The Parish Pastoral Council

I considered different titles for this chapter. I thought of calling it 'The Parish Leadership Group' or 'The Parish Team', terms that might better capture the nature of the group. But 'Parish Pastoral Council' (PPC) is the official name. All the same, it could be a useful exercise for the PPC to ask itself; if we had to choose another name, what might it be?

Among the various ministry groups in today's parish, the PPC is the most significant, or at least it is meant to be. This is not meant in any 'superior' sense. There are three reasons. One is that it has a central role in coordinating and initiating. The second is that, with the number of priests declining, such a group is going to become more and more indispensable.

But the third reason is the most important. The third reason involves the kind of group the PPC is. It is not just another group that simply slots smoothly into the pre-existing set-up. It is part of a new set-up and a different way of doing things. It is part of a different way of seeing parish. It is part of the church's new way of seeing itself. It is part of being an evangelising parish, an every member ministry parish.

I used the phrase 'more indispensable' above. In many parishes the PPC is still far from being indispensable. If it stopped functioning people would hardly notice, and things would just go on as before. This is because the PPC has not yet found its niche. Perhaps it is being grafted on to an old way of seeing and doing things. And the graft does not take.

It is almost inevitable that PPCs will struggle to become established. It takes time to grow into the role. It is still new and un-familiar. This is another reason for hesitating about what to call the group. We do not want to set it in stone when it is so new. We need to leave room for it to evolve, to allow it to take different shapes. We need to explore different models, and to learn from that experience.

What follows in this chapter is an attempt to articulate the current wisdom. The chapter is made up of three 'mini-chapters', to best accommodate all that needs to be discussed. The first of these discusses the role of the PPC. The second is about the spirit and spirituality of the group. The third illustrates what the PPC looks like in operation.

Part One: The Role

Many people on PPCs admit to being unclear about the role. It is not unusual for somebody to be on a council for six months or a year, or longer still, and still be confused as to what it is all about. Maybe it has to do with a deficiency in the initiation at the time of joining. It also has to do with how new the PPC structure still is. It takes a long time to get our heads around it. This is not so much because it is complicated in itself, as that it is part of a new way of seeing ourselves as church.

So, clarifying the role of the PPC begins with the question, 'why?' Why do we have PPCs in the first place? Some people think that it is linked to there being less priests. Interestingly, people had a similar thought when ministers of the Eucharist were introduced. In both cases it is a misunderstanding. The PPC is not there to fill a gap. It stands on its own two feet. It makes sense even if there are just as many priests as ever. The misunderstanding comes from presuming it is part of the older way of seeing church.

A Statement in Itself

Before delving into what the PPC does, we have to reflect on its very existence. The fact that it exists is a statement in itself. PPCs were introduced by the Vatican Council in the 1960s. They were not there before that and are still at an early stage of development in this country. That council, as discussed, was about a new way of seeing ourselves as church. The PPC is part of that, and without it, it makes little sense.

The 'revolution' of Vatican II was from a clerical church to a people's church, from seeing church as a clerical institution to seeing it as a participative community of the people of God. The PPC (along with the diocesan pastoral council) gives structural expression to the church's new way of seeing itself.

The PPC is a structure whereby the members of the faith community share the responsibility for the life, the well-being and the future of their community. In the clerical church all that was taken care of by the clergy. A PPC would not have made sense, except perhaps as a help to the priest in *his* ministry. But it is much more than that, because the PPC is part of a different kind of church.

It can happen that there is a council in the parish, but that the priest, or parishioners, or both, have not entered into the new mindset. The priest may see it as no more than a sounding board, while he continues to hold the reins of power. Or, with less priests, people may see the PPC as doing some of the 'providing for' that the priest used to do. But in a people's church, the PPC is not there to help the priest or fill in for the priest. And it is not there to do things for a passive 'laity' either.

Before elaborating on the role, it will be helpful to note in passing some other things that the PPC is *not*. It is not there to 'run the parish'. It does have a role in keeping an eye on things, but the day-to-day, week-to-week running of the parish is the responsibility of others. Some parishes have a smaller team which meets weekly or fortnightly for this.

Again, the PPC's concern is not finance, maintenance, or administration. Initially many parishes went down that road. It was a kind of division of labour, where the priest did the spiritual work and they did the practical. But, when the church changed the name from 'parish council' to 'parish *pastoral* council', this stressed the pastoral focus of the group.

And the PPC is not a representative group in the parliamentary sense, with its members representing different ministries or parish areas. In the past some PPCs were composed in this way, but it was found to make for a constituency mindset, with people looking out for their own interests. While the PPC is meant to be truly representative of the whole parish, it goes about this in a different way today.

I want to reflect on three words that go a long way towards clarifying what the role of the PPC is: care; planning; leadership. These three words gather together much of what we have learned so far.

CARE

'Parish Pastoral Council' is a cumbersome title. 'Parish Council' would have been simpler. But the word 'pastoral' is very import-ant, even if we tend to slide past it without too much thought. The word is about care, as in the image of the good shepherd – except that the image of sheep and flock does not reflect today's way of seeing church!

People who are members of a PPC are there because they care. They care for the parish. They see the parish as more than a 'plant' or a structure. They see their role as more than a job or a task. It is personal. The parish is people, a community of faith. Being on the PPC is motivated by a care for those people.

It is an overall care, a care for all. That is why the representative model I mentioned is not quite right. Most PPC members are already involved in some parish group or ministry. But when they come on the PPC they take off that hat. Now they represent the whole parish. Their care is for all, their focus is the overall picture.

That is also why the PPC cannot allow itself to be sucked into the nitty-gritty of parish life and ministry. It could, for instance, become absorbed with liturgy, or with communications, or some specific project. If so, then it is losing its way. It is losing its focus on the overall. Different parish groups are there to care for different aspects of the life of the faith community. The PPC is there to exercise overall care.

Growing in Care

It is not just that PPC members are there because they care for the parish, however. Being a member is also a commitment to *grow* in care. PPC meetings are usually monthly. Growing in care means that, when I come to the meeting, I come with a deeper care than the last time. The time in between meetings is time for growing in care. I may or may not have been active in some subgroup or PPC project. But growing in care is meant to be going on all the time.

The main way this happens is through prayer. Of course, the things we do will deepen our care. But I may not always be doing something. Prayer however is constant, ongoing. Here I am not talking about the prayer that happens at meetings. That will be discussed below. Here I am thinking of the prayer that goes on *between* meetings.

I recall some research that was done on how our prayers are answered. It was about people who pray regularly for their partner. What the research discovered was that, when we pray for the other person, *we ourselves* change. We ourselves become more tolerant, more forgiving, more generous, more loving, more grateful, more thoughtful. When we pray for another person, we ourselves become more caring.

The same applies to PPC members. If, between meetings, they take the time to pray for the faith community, they themselves will change. Then, when they come to the next meeting, they will be different. They will bring a more caring self. This is quite the opposite of what happens when the work is hardly thought about between meetings.

So, PPC members can make the parish and its people part of their daily prayer. They can think of who is out there and what might be going on in their lives – young or old, rich or poor, happy or sad, thriving or struggling, serene or bitter, open or closed, and so on. Such prayer raises awareness of others, and awareness generates care. The PPC might put together some resources to help the members grow into this practice of prayer.

Earlier I used a phrase about the parish: 'We care that you exist.' When PPC members pray between meetings, they make this true for themselves. Then the caring parish we have been talking about is 'represented' by the PPC. The PPC stands for the caring parish we aspire to. All its efforts are focused around, and inspired by, care.

PLANNING

Caring is 'soft' language, whereas planning is 'hard' language. The two go together in the case of the PPC. It exercises its care through planning. The distinction between the 'strategic' and the 'operational' is useful here. The PPC is mainly focused on the strategic. Its energy goes into planning ahead rather than into the day-to-day operation of the parish. This is its overall care; not so much the specifics, but the bigger picture, the longer term.

Strategy can sound too much like business language. In fact, it is originally military language. The word is from the Greek for an army commander. From a vantage point, the general takes in the overall picture of what is happening on the battlefield and, from this, identifies the key moves which will bring victory.

Similarly, the strategic role of the PPC is about identifying the key steps that will bring the faith community to where it wants to go. But it is important to stress that strategy has a spiritual meaning here. A good word for it is discernment. Strategic planning is where the PPC thoughtfully and prayerfully seeks to be guided by the Spirit towards discerning what it would be best for the parish to concentrate on.

But the strategic role gets lost if the council becomes too practical, if it is sucked in to the operational, the running of the parish, the nitty-gritty of parish life. When that happens, there is nobody looking at the overall picture. There is nobody planning ahead. Changing times make the strategic role really crucial. If the role is not developed, then the parish will not be responding creatively to its situation.

A Plan of Work

But PPCs struggle to move into a planning mode. What often happens is more like 'hopping' than planning. The PPC begins its term. People want to do something; they do not want to be a talk shop. So they look for something that deserves to be done. When that is completed, they look around again … and so on. After a while they find that they are just hopping from one project to another. Each one is worthy individually, but there is no pattern, no direction, no prioritising. There is no plan. It becomes frustrating.

Part of the problem actually lies in doing things! It is not the role of the PPC to be doing things. Its job is to 'get things done'. The planning role is about identifying what is of priority importance – and then mobilising a response from among the community. It is a different kind of doing. What the PPC does is to ensure that the right issues are being addressed. That requires thinking, discerning, praying, prioritising, planning.

What is needed, rather than hopping from project to project, is a plan of work. One model of a plan of work is where the PPC takes a theme for the year. The theme would be closely related to what tomorrow's parish is all about – themes like those above, such as 'Welcome', or 'Care'. Whatever is chosen would have depth and be able to inspire. A number of different projects to be implemented over the course of the year would be agreed upon.

Another model is a plan of work where a small number of priorities are carefully discerned. These will be the focus of the PPC for most of its term of office, extending over two years or more. The time is divided into blocks, anything from three to six months each. For each block there is a manageable set of projects and targets, designed to address the chosen priorities.

The value of a plan of work should be apparent. There is a sense of direction. There is a map. There is a structure to the work. At the same time it is not set in stone. Once the plan is agreed, the initial projects can be planned in detail. But there is also ongoing review of how it is going. Subsequent stages can be tweaked or revised in light of the experience.

As an image for this, imagine driving along at night. The lights light up the road to the next bend. And that is all that the driver is concentrated on. But the driver also has a destination, a mental map. It is in the background, but it is there. Similarly, the PPC, at any given time, will be focused on some particular project. But it will have its overall plan in the background. It knows that this specific activity is part of something. And that is satisfying, unlike hopping from one action to another with no plan.

The crucial element in a plan of work is discerning the overall priorities, theme or focus. Imagine posing the question; Over the next few years, what, more than anything else, would make a real difference to our faith community? To come to a good answer, the PPC needs to listen, to be in touch with the reality of where people are at. It needs to be in touch with the vision of what we aspire to as parish. Out of this it begins to discern the path.

In comparison to this, we can see how the hopping PPCs tend to do can short-circuit the planning process. It goes straight to doing. It bypasses the listening, the visioning, the discerning. Hopping lacks the direction and the depth that come from a committed process of discernment.

Mobilising

The role of the faith community in the process needs to be emphasised. If only the PPC is involved, then there is no owner-ship. However good it may be, it is merely 'their plan'. Planning is meant to take place in the context of, and in the spirit of, every member ministry. That asks for a substantial engagement with the faith community, consulting people about what is proposed, listening to views and concerns, taking feedback on board. Then people will have a sense of the plan being their own.

Implementing a plan successfully hinges on mobilising people. The PPC formulates a plan of work, then it mobilises others to carry it out. It is a kind of marrying of needs with gifts. The PPC identifies the needs, then it calls for the gifts in the faith community to respond to these needs. So two aims are at work in tandem; achieving specific targets *and* activating every member ministry.

Part of the mobilising will be working with existing groups. The PPC has to gather them around a vision, to establish the 'jigsaw' we spoke of earlier. It enables each of them to see their part in implementing the plan and realising the vision. But a big part of it is also to mobilise new gifts in response to new needs. And it is not good enough for the PPC to do something itself because nobody else volunteered. Its principle should be along the lines that nothing is done until gifts are discovered and people come forward.

A relationship with the parish finance committee is also important. Plans have financial implications. So the finance committee has a significant role in sourcing or generating the resources needed. Part of a good relationship here is about the committee looking beyond the financial, to become familiar with the pastoral planning that is at work.

LEADING

To speak of the PPC in terms of overall care and planning for the parish is to see it in a leadership role. The PPC is not just another ministry group. It is different. It is meant to be the parish leadership team. In the clerical church, the parish priest was the leader. In the people's church, the leadership group is the PPC, with the parish priest as its president.

This is new, and takes getting used to. Members have to grow into it. Often, when the PPC is described in leadership terms, there is resistance. This is quite understandable, because when people think of leadership in the church context they often think of authority and power, subservience and obedience. Members do not want to be seen, or to see themselves, as wielding power and exercising authority.

But this is a different kind of leadership. It draws its inspiration from the Gospel. There, leadership is about service, not power. Jesus says to his disciples, 'You know that the rulers of the Gentiles lord it over them, and their great ones are tyrants over them. It will not be so among you; but whoever wishes to be great among you must be your servant ... just as the Son of Man came not to be served but to serve' (Matthew 20:25–8).

In this Gospel spirit, the PPC's leadership is at the service of the faith community. But service does not mean just 'doing things' for the community. It means enabling the community to become itself, to grow into its own identity. The real leader here is the Spirit; the teacher is Christ. The PPC seeks to facilitate the faith community's journey towards what it is meant to be.

Vision is central to such leadership. The PPC 'holds the vision', the kind of vision articulated in this book. It is inspired and energised by the vision. If not, it has little to offer. And, thus energised and inspired, it leads by enthusing others, by spreading the energy, by mobilising the faith community around the vision; the vision that is its identity and its calling.

We have already touched on this kind of leadership. The PPC leads when it cares for and supports the parish ministry groups, and when it unites them around the vision. It leads when it consults the faith community, when it listens to people and invites people into ownership. When this kind of thing happens, it is not the priest who is in charge of the parish. It is not the PPC that is in charge of the parish. It is the parish that is in charge, assuming responsibility for itself.

This is the kind of leadership that the PPC is called to. It is leadership in the service of every member ministry. So we could say that the role of the PPC – in its caring, its planning, its leading – is to bring into being a truly ministering parish, where every member ministers and is ministered to, where each one evangelises and is evangelised.

Images

Some images may help clarify the kind of leadership the PPC exercises. One image is that of a navigator. Everybody on board has their particular role in sailing the ship. The navigator plots the best route, setting markers to determine overall progress, ensuring all know where they are going. In similar fashion, the PPC 'navigates' the parish, keeping an eye on the overall picture, plotting the course on which all are engaged together.

Another image is that of a midwife. It is the mother who has the baby, not the midwife. The midwife is there to accompany and assist and reassure. But it is not the midwife's process. Likewise in the parish; it is the faith community's own process. The PPC 'leads' by guiding and encouraging people along the path towards a participative faith community.

A third image sees the PPC as the engine. The engine drives the car forward. It gives movement and momentum. Like an engine, the PPC gets the faith community moving forward. Its presence and activity is a propulsion for others. It initiates. It generates energy.

These images put the emphasis firmly on every member ministry. This is not the provided-for parish; it is the ministering community. At the same time, the PPC also 'takes a lead'. It takes responsibility. It makes decisions. But its priority is that the faith community engages as much as possible, and is active as much as possible, in carving out its own future.

Part Two – The 'How'

The attention of the PPC is focused on what it is doing, the task at hand. But no less important than the 'what' is the 'how'. I refer here to how the PPC is as a group; the ethos, the quality of relationships, the spirit and the spirituality. It is far more likely that this 'how' will be neglected than the 'what'. It can even be completely missed. And yet, if the 'how' is not right, the 'what' will struggle, and the group will find it hard to be effective.

This section discusses different aspects of how the group is as a group. Ideally, what is being set out here should be addressed right from the beginning when the group is being set up. It is an essential part of the group's formation. It sets the right tone from the start. It sets the expectations that the group has of itself as a

THE PARISH PASTORAL COUNCIL

group. It is quite difficult to address these issues later on, when bad habits may have been picked up and poor ways of relating may have set in.

A good question to begin with is this; is the PPC a team or a committee? The word 'council' suggests a committee, like the city council or the county council. A committee works through meetings, with an agenda and procedures and voting and so on. 'Team', as in a football team, suggests something quite different. There are as few meetings as possible; the real action takes place elsewhere.

We tend to think of the PPC as a committee. But we would do well to think of it less as a committee and more as a team. Obviously it is a bit of both. Since it operates mainly through the monthly meeting, it is a committee. But it would make a big difference to inject more of a team mentality. This would put the emphasis on the work done outside meetings. But most importantly, it would place more importance on the 'how'. Think of phrases like 'team spirit'. Team spirit can make all the difference.

In the case of the PPC, there is a further dimension. It is made up of people of faith. They have come together to do the work of the Lord, to help build the body of Christ. The way they operate has to reflect who they are. Who they are has to be evident in *how* they are as a group. Ultimately, being on the PPC is itself an experience of being the body of Christ. How members relate to each other has to be an example in itself of the kind of faith community they want to build.

The following are different aspects of what is involved in this. The topics we will address are: the group taking care of itself; the quality of participation; the quality of listening; appreciating gifts; building trust, praying together; the style of decision making. These are specific ways in which the group grows stronger as a group.

TAKING CARE OF OURSELVES

If the people in a parish group enjoy being together, they will do good work. If they enjoy each other's company, if they look forward to it, they will find that the work is more than a chore. But this will not come about automatically. It necessitates that the group pays attention to itself. Groups that fixate on the task miss this and flounder as a result.

What is required is straightforward. First, there needs to be some team building, getting to know each other, becoming comfortable with each other and comfortable with the role. Then there has to be ongoing attention to this. For instance there could be an occasional cup of tea, or even a cup of tea before or after each meeting. Again, I am thinking of at least one social occasion each year, and of occasional time away for prayer.

It is like the proverb, 'all work and no play makes Jack a dull boy'. If there is the work and nothing more, the work itself will weigh people down. The group might even appoint one or two of its members to take a responsibility here. Their job would be simply to ensure that the group is caring for itself in an ongoing way.

'Checking in' is a useful part of the caring process. Once or twice a year, the chairperson invites everyone to say how they are finding things. It might be that nothing comes up and that everybody is content. It is worth it just to find out that. But it might be that some are not so content. Maybe the meetings never start on time; or some are dominating and others feel left out; or the prayer is rushed; or the agenda is never completed. The check-in is a kind of safety valve, to release tension that could otherwise build up and do damage.

MAXIMISING PARTICIPATION

A second aspect of the 'how' is about maximising the quality of participation across all the members of the group. In a typical group some people do most of the talking; a few more do a bit of talking; some others say little, or nothing at all. That is the default mode of a group; meaning that it will stay like that unless something is done to change it.

This is not about making people talk, though it may involve making other people stop talking so much! The quiet people in the group are often the ones who do the most listening and thinking, while there are others who talk before they think at all. The danger with the default position is that some people will feel that they are not taking part.

It is maddening when some people dominate the discussion. It goes totally against team spirit. Nobody's views matter so much that they should be the only ones heard. What does matter is that all the gifts in the group are being brought into play. Everybody is there for a reason. Everybody has to feel that they make a difference to the group. If care is not taken, some people may come to feel that it does not matter if they are there or not.

I referred to John Paul II's phrase a 'spirituality of communion'. He talked about 'the ability to see what is positive in others, to welcome and prize it as a gift from God'.[41] This is team spirit. The welcoming disposition towards each other maximises participation. With it, all feel that their presence is appreciated and their contributions valued.

There are techniques that can help. The chairperson can pause a discussion and ask people to talk in pairs about the topic. Many people find it easier to talk one-to-one than to speak to a group. If, in pairs, one person affirms what the other says, then confidence is boosted and there is a stronger inclination to share their thoughts with the full group.

LISTENING TO EACH OTHER

The quality of listening is crucial to the quality of participation. It is not unusual for people to be so intent on getting their own point in that they do not hear what others are saying. Maybe it is part of the council or committee mentality, trying to ensure that one's own view prevails. It means that points are being piled up, one on another. Promising contributions end up buried. People end up frustrated or hurt.

The goal is not that somebody's view wins out. It is that we hear God's Spirit. The belief is that God's Spirit speaks in and through each of us and that, if we listen to one another, we will also hear what the Spirit is saying to us. If we have this belief, then when others are speaking we will clear our minds and make a welcoming space in our hearts for what others want to say.

Members need to commit themselves to learning the art of listening. We are not necessarily the good listeners we would like to think we are! We all have our prejudices. We all make presumptions. We hear what we want to hear and miss what was actually said. We can close ourselves to hearing. We can dismiss someone or their views. But, if we practise being good listeners at all times, then we will bring that with us to the group.

It will make a difference if group members also watch out for each other. It can happen that somebody says something and it is not heard or taken up by the group. If someone else notices this happening, that person can intervene and draw the group's attention back to what it missed, to listen attentively this time. We each listen out for not-listening!

APPRECIATING GIFTS

Everybody brings something to the group and everybody has something to offer. People do not always know what it is that they have to offer. Many people lack confidence in themselves. They think they have little to offer, nothing to contribute. But if there is team spirit, and if participation is being maximised, and if people are listening well, then all the gifts can come into play. People will become more confident about themselves. People will discover what they have to offer. Each will grow to appreciate what others bring to the table.

The group will also learn the value of a balance of gifts. One balance that comes up often is between doers and thinkers. Both are needed and each needs to appreciate the other. There is the balance between tradition and innovation, between new faces and familiar faces, between energy and wisdom. Each group can come to identify where it is strong and where it is falling short. Then it can go about making up for what is lacking.

There is a good exercise for growing in appreciation. When the members are familiar with one another, set aside forty minutes or so during a meeting. Divide the group in two. The people in each group spend about ten minutes talking about the gifts of the people in the other group, two minutes per person. Each one writes on a card what was said about one of the people from the other group. Then the groups come together and each person speaks about a person from the other group. At the end, each person is given their card.

A CLIMATE OF TRUST

Trust is something that is earned by the group. It comes from people getting to know one another. It comes from each having a feeling of participation and knowing that their presence matters. It comes from a spirit of listening and from the feeling of mutual respect that brings. It comes from a spirit of appreciation where individuals feel affirmed in the giftedness they bring to the group. With these foundations, people can feel secure about who they are in one another's eyes.

When this trust is built up, the group will be strong in times of difficulty. When disagreements and tensions arise, there will be a spirit within the group that is able to cope with them. The mutual respect of the members makes a good outcome much more likely. But if the group has not taken care of itself – has not fostered its team spirit and the quality of participation, listening and mutual appreciation – then trust will be weak. There will not be the resources to draw on when difficulties come.

One practical move towards building a climate of trust is an agreement about the confidentiality of group discussions. That will help give people the freedom and security to participate openly. With a climate of trust, people can explore. They can think out loud without the fear of being ridiculed. They can say something that turns out to be silly without the fear that it is going to be spread abroad. Members know that each one's heart is in the right place.

TIME FOR PRAYER

We spoke above about the prayer between meetings, helping the members grow in their care for the parish. Here we look at the prayer that takes place at the meeting. It is a very important part of the 'how'. Praying together is central to how the PPC members are as a group.[42]

Prayer at meetings can be poor. There may be a quick prayer to get the meeting going, a kind of nod in the direction of God. It is like the referee blowing the whistle to start the game: 'quickly and we're off!' And even when it is a little longer, maybe a reflection or a reading, it can still be in the mode of 'saying a prayer' or 'reading a reading'. What we are talking about here is different. It is about an *experience* of praying together as a group.

The prayer may be at the start of the meeting, or it may be in the middle. It can be quite short or it can be more extended. But longer does not necessarily mean better. Whether it is three minutes or ten minutes, it is the quality of the prayer time that matters. Ideally it would be prepared in turn by different members of the group (in pairs, if that helps). It will include some quiet time. Usually a text is read out and there is an opportunity to share thoughts or prayers. There may be a sacred space to focus attention.

It would be worthwhile for the group to chat over two questions, to help people get into a way of praying together. One question is; why is this prayer time together important? The other question is; why might people find it difficult?

The prayer is important for a few reasons. It puts the work in a context, highlighting that it is God's work and that God's Spirit is the heart of team spirit. It helps bond the group in a shared faith vision. It helps the group to 're-collect' itself, bringing the members back to who they are and what they are about. It allows them to bring their experience, highs and lows, successes and struggles, into a sacred place of comfort and challenge.

And there are reasons why people might find this difficult. A lot of people are used to saying prayers, or even meditating, on their own, but are unfamiliar with praying with others. People may feel inadequate or incompetent, especially as regards leading the prayer. They may think that it is the priest's job, not theirs. They may not see its value. They may think that it is eating up valuable meeting time.

The aim, I propose, is for all members to come to the point where they agree that prayer is the heart of the meeting. But it takes time to get to that. It has to be taken gently, at people's own pace, so that it is comfortable. It probably requires a 'training' session on the practicalities of how to go about it. And it requires periodic review, to ensure that the experience continues to be enriching.

CONSULTATION AND DECISION MAKING

When it comes to the PPC making a decision on something, how it goes about it is as important as what it actually decides. This again is part of its team spirit and the spirituality of partnership. If it were just a regular council or committee, decisions might be arrived at through a vote. The mentality could be one of winning, of one's own view prevailing. But that is not how it is meant to be here. The way the PPC makes decisions comes out of its spirit of participation and trust, of listening and mutual appreciation.

This spirit makes for a consensus style of decision-making. Yet that does not seem to square with what the church says about the PPC having a 'consultative' voice.[43] That word sounds as if the PPC is no more than advisory to the parish priest. Alas, in some places the word is taken up in this way.

Consultation

But there is more to it. 'Consultation' has two levels of meaning; one of them legal, the other pastoral. At the legal level, it reflects the status of the parish priest in canon law. He is appointed by the bishop to the care of the parish. He is responsible to the bishop; the buck stops with him. That is his position and he cannot divest himself of it. We need to acknowledge the legal set-up for what it is, and then concentrate on the *pastoral* meaning of consultation.

The pastoral sense is about a people's church, a participative faith community, where the Spirit shines in each person. It is about a church of every member ministry. The PPC is an expression of this kind of church, a symbol of it. It seeks to be the kind of faith community it aspires to build. Its team spirit is itself a spirit of consultation.

In this sense, consultation is part of a search for the truth. When I consult you about a problem or issue, I am looking for the truth. I consult you because I think you may be able to enlighten my

THE PARISH PASTORAL COUNCIL

search. Of course, it may be that I have my mind made up already. Or it may be that I will only listen if you say certain things. But consultation at its best means listening in an open spirit, ready to take on board what is said. The Spirit is in charge.

When the PPC is exploring some issue and working towards a decision, it is looking for the truth. It wants to hear what the Spirit is saying. It finds this in the collective wisdom of the group. The Spirit is in each member and speaks through each one. So the best way of hearing the Spirit is by listening to each person. If we fail to listen, we may fail to hear what the Spirit is saying.

Consensus

Consultation in this pastoral sense is expressed in a consensus style of decision-making. To illustrate, imagine the group deliberating on when to hold a parish open day. Some strong voices are advocating the Autumn; one or two quieter types timidly suggest Spring; others again have not spoken. The facilitator asks for a comment, one by one, from everybody, to get a sense of the overall. When that is done, it emerges that most people actually favour a Spring date.

Consensus is first of all about listening to everybody. It is about the equality of quieter voices and dominant voices. The first step in consensus is knowing that everybody has been heard. Now the Spirit has been released. It is clear from the example how this might never have happened, and how, without taking the time to listen, the views of a few could have been mistaken for the collective wisdom of all.

The next step is taking each other seriously. There will be majority voices and minority voices. If I am in a minority and the majority take me seriously, I am inclined to take the majority seriously in turn. But taking each other seriously may mean retracing ground, going back over why some people see things differently. It means ensuring that minority voices feel heard.

The final stage is not unanimity, but consensus. One or two may end up saying, 'I don't agree with the majority view, but I'm happy that I have been listened to, and I'm happy to go along with the consensus.' Note the language. It is not that 'I'll reluctantly and resentfully give way'. It is that 'I'm happy to go with this'. Consensus does not leave people feeling ignored or defeated. It is about a 'win-win', not 'win-lose'. People are happy that the process was right, the 'how' we decide working for the benefit of all.

THE PRIEST

Where does the priest stand in all this? In the chapter on 'who's who' I spoke of his facilitative role, activating the participation of others. Likewise here, he encourages the processes of consultation, listening and participation. That, of course, includes his own participation, contributing his own views. When a consensus is emerging, his role is one of affirming the decision. It is about acknowledging the working of the Spirit in the working of the group.

What, though, if the priest is the minority voice and seems to stand against the rest of the group? In that case consensus is lacking in a special way. Again we follow the way outlined; retracing our steps, listening again. Someone put it in a way I find helpful. The priest should be slow to act against the consensus of the rest of the group, and the group should be reluctant to move ahead without the priest being on board.

People sometimes fear that there is a power of veto at play. In a sense there is; there is no getting away from the priest's canonical position. But if the process is right, questions of a veto do not arise. If the group takes care of itself and nurtures the team spirit of participation, listening, appreciation, trust, consultation, then there need be no fear. They can be confident of arriving at the truth – together.

The Parish

There is a further and essential dimension to the processes of consultation and decision-making – the parish dimension. In the clerical church, the priest decided for the people. But in a people's church, that is not to be replaced by the PPC making decisions for the parish. That would still be a clerical style of church. Rather, a people's church works towards a situation where the faith community takes ownership.

The PPC is not deciding *for* the parish; it is making decisions *on behalf of* the parish. So the spirit of consultation has to extend to the faith community. That is not easy. There is at least some level of passivity, the conditioning of generations of not having a voice. The PPC has to build up a culture of consultation and co-responsibility and ownership. This is part of its role of facilitating every member ministry.

Ongoing communication will help build this culture. There can be frequent reference to the work of the PPC at Sunday Eucharist. There can be an occasional presentation by the chairperson. PPC members can greet people at the door on special occasions. All this makes for good visibility for the PPC.

There might be a parish assembly every year or two, to review, to listen, to present plans and receive feedback. In between, there can be specific gatherings to consult people on particular issues. Alongside this there would be ongoing communication with the parish groups, and the various media and social media would be used to keep people in the loop.

Communication is more than giving out information and telling people what is going on. That is too passive. It is about inviting people in, activating their ownership. It is about putting the *idea* of the PPC out there, the idea of a participative faith community. It is about empowering people, making it possible for them to engage.

Part Three – The Life Cycle

This section goes through a PPC 'life cycle'. It goes from the initial setting up of a PPC through the term of office. This is in order to give a 'picture' of what the PPC looks like in practice. Obviously, it is only a model. Each PPC can relate it to its own actual situation.

STRUCTURE

The term of office is usually three years. Meetings are usually monthly, about ten in the year. The optimum size of the group is between ten and fifteen members, small enough for good team participation and big enough to go well when some cannot be present. The aim is to have a balance of age, gender, and different experiences. A facility for co-option can help with this.

If, when the PPC completes its term, a new group is put in place, it helps continuity if two or three of the former group stay on for a year. But continuity can also be ensured by a regular, ongoing rollover of membership. For example, each year one third of the group could retire and be replaced.

In a small number of parishes, the group meets more frequently, perhaps twice a month. This tends to mean that the group becomes more involved in the operational side of the parish. To avoid losing sight of the planning role, such groups could alternate meetings between operational and strategic agendas.

RECRUITMENT

What matters in recruiting is getting the right people for the job; there are 'horses for courses'. That includes having a good mix of people. It would be good for the parish to articulate what qualities it expects of each and every member within that mix, for instance:

❖ In a position to give the time needed.

❖ Able to think in terms of the whole parish rather than any particular interest.

❖ A team player, able to work well with others and to listen.

❖ Open to new ways of doing things; willing to explore.

❖ Able to work by way of meetings; reflecting, planning, reviewing.

❖ A faith full of energy and passion for the future of the faith community.

❖ Open to formation, at the beginning and ongoing.

Recruiting can be seen in two stages. The first stage would be some form of personal discernment and self-selection, following on good information about what is being sought. Individuals can be encouraged one-to-one, but the motivation has to come from themselves. A second stage would be some form of parish discernment, to ensure a good mix of people. This could involve a parish assembly, where those who come forward are presented to the faith community.

The time of recruiting is an opportunity to build up more awareness of the PPC and its significance. There could be a talk at Mass about its role and about the pastoral situation today. This would be part of an ongoing effort to bring people on board and to build ownership of the vision that the PPC stands for.

GETTING STARTED

If there is regular rollover of membership, getting started need only happen once, unless circumstances call for a new start and a new group. Getting started takes time. It is like laying the foundations when building a house. Those joining the PPC may be unfamiliar with what is involved and with the thinking behind it. So, if the 'forming' stage is rushed through, everything that follows will suffer the consequences.

Serious attention to formation is required, considering what is needed at this point. Time is needed for team building. Members need to be familiarised with the role of the PPC. They need to grow in a shared vision, the kind that this book has been setting out. They need the theology and spirituality to underpin their involvement. They need to look at the 'how' we have discussed in this chapter, to set the tone for their time as a group.

Choosing the chairperson and secretary deserves careful thought. Secretary is easier, and it can be made more attractive if the position is rotated every six or twelve months. The chairperson can be chosen once people know each other well enough to judge. There are two requirements. First, this person has to be able to prepare a good agenda and move through it efficiently. Second, he or she is as much a facilitator as a chairperson, able to enable, setting a standard as regards listening and respect and participation.

Getting started continues over a number of months. The new group has to be introduced to the faith community, perhaps with a commissioning ritual.[44] It has to initiate contact with the parish ministry groups. All of this matters a lot, because it gets the group's relationship with the parish off to a good start. Often PPCs remain anonymous and invisible. They need to have a strong profile in the parish.

In order to move into planning, the group also needs to listen at this stage. Usually each member has a limited knowledge of all that goes on in the parish. All need to be familiarised with the overall picture of where the parish is at. This includes the demographics, the extent of what is currently happening, the issues, the challenges, the strengths and weaknesses.

In relation to vision, the parish may or may not have a mission statement or a vision statement. If it does, the statement may need to be resuscitated or updated. If the parish has no such statement, it could be good to make it part of the group's workload in these early stages. If this is made into a consultative and participative process, it could be a useful part of engaging with the faith community.

A PLAN

I have already given some ideas about the structure of a plan of work. It is a key part of the first six months. The better quality time given to it, the better the plan will be. When it is done, the PPC has a map. It has worked out its focus. It has identified projects and targets for the immediate future. The work has a shape and a structure. There is no hopping around!

Listening and visioning feed into this. But formulating the plan of work should involve the faith community. The PPC might come up with a draft for discussion. This can be revised in the light of feedback and presented back to the parish for ratification. In this way the spirit of consultation extends beyond the PPC itself to embrace the whole parish.

A quick win is important. The early months are about establishing a good foundation and formulating a promising plan of work. But it will boost the spirits of the group if it also completes some modest project early on. The could be a gathering of the ministry groups, for instance; or it could be a vision statement; or some other modest project.

Meetings and Subgroups

The PPC works through meetings. But there are options as to how the meeting and its agenda are structured. Consider the following three models:

(a) The traditional agenda; prayer, minutes, matters arising from the minutes, correspondence, item one, item two, and so on, concluding with 'any other business'.

(b) A one-item agenda, about an important topic or project. A subgroup researches and presents at the meeting. Then there is discussion, then time for prayer, and after prayer a decision may be made. Following this, there is time for other business.

(c) A mix of (a) and (b). The meeting is in two parts. One half is devoted to an extended discussion of some major topic, perhaps with a subgroup presentation as above. Or it could be a formation time for the group. The other half is for other agenda items as in the first model above.

These are only possible formats. But I think it is fair to say that, for the PPC to enter into its planning role, it needs to move away from exclusive reliance on model (a). It needs to utilise the other models as well, depending on what is most appropriate. In particular, PPCs need to free themselves from slavery to a business agenda and make more time for reflective, in-depth discussion. So model (c) might merit exploration. Or there might be a few meetings during the year along the lines of model (b), in place of model (a).

The use of subgroups makes the PPC more effective. Subgroups have two roles. One is preparing for a meeting. If, for example, the PPC wants to set up a Baptism team, it makes sense for some people to go and research it, find out the best practice. The discussion will then be informed, instead of people pooling their ignorance.

The other role is in following through from a meeting. Taking the same example, if the PPC decides to set up a Baptism team, the next step is not to do it themselves, but to mobilise a response. A couple of interested members could work on setting up a team.

They might accompany the new group for a while, but then leave it go. In this way, PPC subgroups would be short-term and members would not be drawn away from the PPC's proper role.

Ongoing Formation

Besides the initial formation emphasised above, the PPC would do well to keep the importance of ongoing formation in mind. Formation is more than an introductory explanation of how to do a job. It is a continuing process of initiation, entering more deeply into the experience. The following three points might be considered.

First, the experience of being on the PPC is itself formative. If the group takes care of itself as described, and if it stays focused on its role, then it will be experiencing (on a smaller scale) the kind of faith community it aspires to build. Members will find their own faith and their own sense of church being enhanced and enriched. If something along those lines is not the case, then the PPC is probably not working as it should be.

Second, it is worth having an annual enrichment session, perhaps mid-year. This would be an opportunity to stand back from the work, to reconnect with the vision, to be re-energised. It could possibly take the form of a mini-retreat. An outside speaker or facilitator could be a big help.

Third, it is important to hold an annual review. In a rollover system, this could be the time for initiating new members (rather than just leaving them to find their feet). The previous year's work could be reviewed and the year ahead surveyed. There would be an element of prayer and an element of enrichment. Through the occasion, the group would be renewing and refreshing itself.

Formation is an appropriate theme with which to conclude this chapter. The PPC is vital to tomorrow's parish. Though introduced in the church over fifty years ago, PPCs are still quite new in Ireland. This chapter will have indicated how much is involved in making them strong and fruitful. But formation is at the heart of it. Initial and ongoing formation are crucial in developing a planning mentality, in ensuring that members grow into the role and in maintaining good practice in working together as a group.

CHAPTER EIGHTEEN
Grouping Parishes Together

The parish in Ireland is entering uncharted waters today due to the decreasing number of priests. There is a need to rationalise, and so parishes are being grouped together into bigger pastoral units. It might be just two parishes with the one parish priest. Or it could be as many as six or seven parishes in a kind of federation, with priests resident in as many of them as possible and operating together as a team.

It is all evolving. There are a lot of logistics involved and there are different ways of structuring the groupings, even within the same diocese. Will most parishes be in groupings, but some parishes merged together? Will the grouping be a federation of parishes or a new 'super parish'? How many parishes should there be in a grouping? How can it be organised so that groupings are natural units? Will there be a parish priest in each parish, or a priest leader in a team of priests? What leadership roles will there be for parishioners and pastoral workers?

Such questions are not the focus here. Rather, what follows is a reflection on how all of this links in with what the book has been discussing. We will be asking, 'how does the grouping of parishes fit in what has been said about tomorrow's parish as an evangelising faith community?'

FAITH COMMUNITIES

In a sense, the phenomenon of grouping is already part of parish life. There are many parishes where there are two or more churches. Until recently there would have been a priest living in each church area, one of them being the parish priest. There might be separate PPCs or one PPC for the whole parish. In these cases, parish can look like an artificial unit, or an administrative unit made up of a number of Eucharistic communities.

In a sense, there is something not unlike this in most parishes. In any parish with just one church, where there are multiple weekend Masses, there are also a number of Eucharistic communities! What is happening now is on a bigger scale. Besides different church areas within the one parish, or different worshipping communities at the same church, we have different parishes within the one larger unit.

What can be taken from this is that, with the new bigger units, the basic unit remains. The basic unit is the Eucharistic community, the people who gather in a particular place to celebrate the Eucharist. Indeed, that is what the New Testament word for church – *ekklesia* – means. It means the gathering. What we call a parish may correspond to one Eucharistic community, or it may comprise multiple communities.

When parishes are being grouped into bigger units, it remains the case that the basic unit is the local faith community, the Eucharistic community. Closing churches is not a desirable option and remains very much a last resort. For the foreseeable future, the focus is on the vitality of the local faith community. A grouping of parishes is not a faith community. It is more an administrative unit comprising multiple faith communities, just as many parishes have been for years. The concern of the grouping has to be about how each Eucharistic community can be the kind of faith community this book has been talking about.

MISSION AND MAINTENANCE

At the same time, the grouping is more than an administrative unit. It helps to look at this through the 'lens' of the oft-quoted contrast between maintenance and mission. Mission refers to the outward thrust, the outreach of the faith community. Maintenance refers to the management of parish life, 'running the parish'. The grouping arrangement concerns both. But on balance, the focus should be mission rather than maintenance.

Sometimes the way we talk about grouping parishes is almost too positive, as if it is simply the right thing to do. We can forget that the current movement towards grouping is born of necessity. It is not the 'right thing' in the sense of something that is desirable in itself. Rather it is the right thing in the sense that it is (or seems to be) the appropriate response to a particular set of circumstances. Talk of grouping only arises because the number of priests is decreasing. We would not be talking about it otherwise.

So, at this level, it is a maintenance issue. How do we keep the show on the road with less priests available? We need to reduce the number of Masses and to rationalise Mass times. Priests on their own in parishes need cover for illness and holidays. There is a need to train parishioners for pastoral roles, such as funeral ministry and leading funeral prayers. At least in part, these are all maintenance issues. Grouping parishes into bigger units (whatever model is adopted) is a reasonable way of addressing them.

But that is all about dealing with necessities. There is also what is called making a virtue of necessity. And that is where we shift from maintenance to mission. This means turning the situation to our advantage – by seeing it as an invitation to evangelise. In this sense, grouping parishes is much more than an administrative affair. Now the question is about how faith communities can collaborate in bigger units to promote the mission of each. It is about how to help one another become the kind of faith community each is meant to be.

FEAR AND RESISTANCE

Change makes for anxiety and insecurity, and that is as true here as anywhere else. People resist change, and the main reason is often that they are afraid of something. This is true both of parishioners and priests.

For those in the faith community who are aware of the grouping process, there is the frequently voiced fear of the parish losing autonomy. People are afraid of independence being lost if the parish is absorbed into a bigger unit. The fear is understandable. Each faith community has its own distinctive identity that makes it what it is. Each has its own personality or charisma. People feel this and they value it, even if they have not put words on what it is exactly. They do not want to lose it.

For priests, it is unfamiliar terrain. They are used to being in charge, each at the helm of his own individual unit. It is more than being in charge though. It is also the special mutual relationship between the priest and a particular faith community. The fear is that this will be lost when he is part of a team overseeing a larger unit. 'Team' itself is also part of the fear. Very many priests are conditioned into and accustomed to a quite an individualistic style of ministry.

Regarding the fears among the faith community, the analogy of a relationship is helpful. When two people start going out together, there is expectation and there is apprehension. Each wants the relationship to be enriching. They do not want to be dominated or suffocated by the other. In a good relationship people become more themselves, not less. Intimacy is for the enhancement of identity, not its suppression.

Grouping parishes is like a new relationship. Each one legitimately asks; how is this going to affect me? If things go well, they will come to see that there is a lot in it for them. They will benefit from doing things together. They will appreciate the mutual support. Their identity will grow stronger. But it hinges on paying attention to the quality of the relationship, getting to know one another, growing in trust.

Regarding priests' fears, priests too are right to ask; how will this affect me? And they too can come to find a lot in the grouping experience. As the number of priests gets fewer and fewer, grouping can address the threat of isolation. It can offer practical support when it comes to holidays and sickness. Equally, it can re-energise priests and give them a new impetus in their calling.

The GAA offers an interesting analogy. There, the club is the basic unit. But some club players go on to play for their county. When that happens there is a twin loyalty, to both club and county. It is possible to be passionate about both and not to feel threatened about either. There is room for both. So, when parishes come together in a good way, passion for one's own faith community can coexist with passion for the grouping.

A Twin-Track Process
In many situations, I think it would be well worthwhile adopting a 'twin-track' approach to the process. One track is where there is a group made up of people (including the priests) from the different faith communities within the grouping. The other track is where the priests of the grouping meet amongst themselves. (That obviously presumes that there are multiple priests, rather than where one priest has responsibility for multiple faith communities.)

At first this might sound a bit suspicious. It has an echo of the clerical church. It sounds like the priests are a kind of inner circle, holding control. So it has to be very clear to all that this is not what is intended. Rather, the idea is that a twin structure is appropriate to the process, and perhaps necessary. The central group is the inter-parish group. That is where the real action takes place, the collaboration in evangelisation. But it is important, alongside this, for the priests to meet on their own.

There are strong reasons for this. For one, there are issues that concern only the priests. The issue of cover has already been mentioned; the priests committing to and organising to fill in for one another when ill or on a break. There is the issue of what the experience is like for them as priests. In sharing their experience they can be encouraged by one another. Another reason is that priests who are reluctant or nervous can 'hide' within the larger inter-parish group, and never buy in. Meeting with their peers makes it more likely that they will commit and become a positive presence in the main group.

One such grouping where an inter-parish group was established comes to mind, where the priests continued to meet among themselves. They met monthly for lunch, then prayed together, then discussed priest-specific issues like those mentioned. After a year or so they were reaping the benefits. There was a new feeling of friendship. There was less feeling of being isolated. They were experiencing support for one another and growing in a spirit of solidarity.

The inter-parish forum, though, is central. The composition of the group can vary. It can include representatives of the PPCs, the priests, parish sisters, pastoral workers, and possibly parish secretaries or others. Its main focus is practical. Just as a couple get to know each other by doing things together, so too shared practical projects are the way to build up inter-parish solidarity.

People can jump straightaway to questions of structure. Are we going to have a 'super PPC' for the grouping? Do we pool our finances? That is like a couple meeting and immediately starting to talk of marriage and joint bank accounts! Those questions can wait till later, maybe much later. Now is about getting to know each other, doing things together, building a relationship, coming to enjoy the friendship.

Examples of practical projects are: joint training for ministries and ministry teams; a joint parish mission; a joint Lenten or Advent exercise; an information directory for the grouping; a name for the grouping. But the emphasis should be more mission than maintenance. Collaboration could come to mean a lot here. For instance, youth ministry and adult faith development are challenges that could be addressed more energetically and creatively by a few parishes together.

THE PARISH PASTORAL COUNCILS

The inter-parish group is not a 'super PPC', though that is something that could be on the agenda later on. The individual PPCs continue, just as the individual faith communities continue to have a life of their own. But the PPCs are a particularly important element in the grouping process. The inter-parish group is a symbol of their partnership. It is vital that they buy into the process, that they engage seriously with it. That includes their engaging with their faith communities too, creating awareness, generating ownership.

As the process develops, the PPC's role becomes more significant. It will be natural for the group of parishes to move beyond collaborating on individual projects and into more of a planning role. That will require the full engagement of the PPCs, in identifying pastoral priorities for the grouping as a whole, and in agreeing upon common policies and standards. The PPC is a planning group, but the grouping of parishes is now an intrinsic part of its planning, not just an added extra.

Planning will, of course, include dealing with the decreasing presence of priests. The leadership role of the PPCs themselves is going to move more centre stage. Leadership figures who are not priests are going to be needed in each faith community.

Addressing all this will be helped by good collaboration between the PPCs. Their collaboration might begin as an annual gathering of all the members of all the PPCs. This would be focused on building the foundations of a good relationship between them.

THE DIOCESE DIMENSION

Meanwhile, there is the diocesan dimension of all this. Grouping is an initiative on the part of the diocese. The diocese needs to play its part in order that parishes can successfully negotiate the new and unfamiliar terrain. Leadership is needed. It will not do to leave parishes just to work it out for themselves.

Leadership here involves articulating a vision and bringing people on board. It involves policymaking. It involves clarifying roles and expectations. It involves providing support and making resources available. It involves taking the experience on board and learning from it, so that the best possible practices and structures can evolve.

There is an opportunity here to bring collaborative ministry to a new level. Each parish tends to go its own way, and that is not necessarily a bad thing. But in times like these, parishes need the energy and encouragement that come from feeling part of something bigger. The diocese can bring that extra dimension. The quality of its leadership can nudge parish groupings forward. It can help overcome reluctance and inject new hope.

A SCRIPTURAL REFLECTION

We all know the phrase, 'God loves a cheerful giver'. It originates from the pen of the apostle Paul, writing to the Christians in Corinth, as he encourages them to contribute generously to the collection for the impoverished church in Jerusalem. In the course of this, he reminds them of the generosity of the Christians in Macedonia towards the same cause (2 Corinthians, chapters 8 and 9). 'Parishes together' is already there in our origins as church.

Paul's appeal reflects his idea of the solidarity there ought to be among Christians in different places. At a time when 'church' meant the local faith community, his initiative was a step towards developing a spirit of unity between communities. This evokes a sense of church as a communion of communities. Paul's words about the body of Christ are apt in this context. 'If one member suffers, all suffer together with it; if one member is honoured, all rejoice together with it' (1 Corinthians 12:26).

We have a contemporary instance of what Paul was doing in the twinning of parishes. Here, a parish from our part of the world twins with a parish in another part of the world, often the developing world. This is in order to share its greater resources with those in more need. But there is a mutual enrichment. There are also some instances of local twinning, where one parish shares its resources with another less fortunate parish within the diocese.

I say all this in order to apply it as a theological reflection on the current grouping of parishes. Though the issue today is not financial, the same spirit of solidarity is at play. It is ironic that the adjective deriving from parish is 'parochial'. A parochial outlook is one that is insular, limited, narrow, inward-looking, even petty and small-minded. And, indeed, parishes have tended to exist in splendid isolation, each a separate kingdom, as it were. In his own way, Paul challenges that. And we can see his challenge today in the challenge that the grouping process poses to the 'parochial' parish.

Paul's practice inspires the idea that a faith community can only fully be itself when it reaches out beyond itself. A parish is only a parish when it not parochial! Thus the grouping of parishes may be bringing out a forgotten dimension of what a parish is. Faith communities are not meant to exist in isolation, but rather as a communion of communities. This is a further dimension of the collaborative ministry we spoke of. It is a further experience of the divine synergy that collaborative ministry is.

It is the same way that people only find themselves by going outside themselves. Identity is achieved in relationship, communion, intimacy. The grouping of parishes can feel like another burden. It can be sensed as a threat. Or it can be seen as an invitation out of isolation and into relationship. And in that context of relationship, each faith community can find itself anew, and grow into the evangelising parish it is called to be.

AFTERWORD

I began this book with an image – that of the motorway. Ireland's recently built motorways have bypassed so many towns and villages that we used to work our way through. Those places symbolise today's parish, bypassed by so many people, no longer on life's itinerary. I want to conclude the book by adding something to that image.

Thinking again of all those places that have been bypassed, there is one that I miss. On the old road from Dublin to Cork, in County Tipperary, there is a long curve. As you come out of the curve, there comes into view the Rock of Cashel. It just stands there, in front of you, the centre of the landscape, an imposing vista, majestic, filled with history and filled with beauty.

The rock is a symbol for our parish. Both have been bypassed, and that is fair enough; people have things to do and places to go. At the same time, the rock is a symbol, not just for something bypassed, but for the wonderful thing we have to offer. There is something here of great value, of great moment.

Yet we are not to take this suggestion with presumption. We should not say, 'ah yes, that's us, that's our parish'. For we are not yet the great thing that the rock symbolises. To think so would amount to a new bout of complacency. Rather, the rock is a symbol of tomorrow, a symbol of tomorrow's parish.

The symbol of the rock is the key to tomorrow's parish. It challenges us to unlock for ourselves what it is that we have, what it is that we are. Yes, I said for ourselves. For the moment, we forget about anybody else. We forget about the 'lapsed', we forget about reaching out. The rock represents what we can rediscover about ourselves.

We are talking about a journey inwards. The rock stands for what it is to be a faith community, a community of disciples, a ministering community. It challenges us to rediscover the bigger picture we are part of. It challenges us to find again what we have probably come to take for granted.

'Out there', on the motorway, people are living lives that are interesting, lives that are worthwhile, lives that are enriching. We thank God for all of them. And we pray for all who do not have that experience of life. And we turn again to our source, our centre, to connect as if for the first time with what it is that we have to offer.

NOTES

1 See Charles Taylor, *A Secular Age* (Harvard University Press, 2007), Introduction.

2 Micheál Mac Gréil, *Pluralism and Diversity in Ireland* (Dublin: Columba, 2011), chapter 17.

3 Grace Davie, *Europe: the Exceptional Case* (London: Darton, Longman and Todd, 2002), 19–20. 'Believing without belonging' is the subtitle of her *Religion in Britain since 1945* (Oxford: Blackwell, 1994).

4 Yann Martel, *The Life of Pi* (Edinburgh: Canongate, 2002), 28.

5 Madeleine Bunting, 'List for Life', *The Tablet*, 23 November 2013, 12–13.

6 See Vatican II, *The Church*, 16; *The Church in the Modern World*, 22.

7 New York: Columbia University Press, 2010.

8 *The Letters and Diaries of Etty Hillesum, 1941–1943* (Grand Rapids: Eerdmans, 2002). A shorter, more accessible version: *An Interrupted Life and Letters from Westerbork* (New York: Holt, 1996).

9 Charles Handy, *The Empty Raincoat* (London: Hutchinson, 1994), 50–4.

10 Based on Isak Dinesen's story, *Anecdotes of Destiny* (London: Penguin, 1986), 21–68.

11 *Collected Poems 1945–1990* (London: Phoenix Grant, 1996), 233.

12 *The Church in the Modern World*, 39.

13 *The Church's Missionary Activity*, 2.

14 Paul VI, *Address to the Roman Clergy*, 24 June 1963; John Paul II, *The Vocation and Mission of the Lay Faithful* (1988), 25–8; Francis, *The Joy of the Gospel* (2013), 28.

15 Johann Baptist Metz, *The Emergent Church* (London: SCM, 1981), 3.

16 Sebastian Barry, *The Secret Scripture* (London: Faber and Faber, 2009), 38.

17 Pius X, *Vehementer Nos* (1906), 8.

18 *The Church*, 10, 31, 34–6.

19 *The Ministry and Life of Priests*, 2.

20 *Ibid.*, 9.

21 *Catechism of the Catholic Church*, 1547.

22 *At the Dawn of a New Millennium* (2001), 43.

23 *Evangelisation in the Modern World* (1975), 14–15.

24 *The Joy of the Gospel*, 120.

25 *Ibid.*, 164.

26 *Evangelisation in the Modern World*, 15.

27 *The Church's Missionary Mandate* (1990), 33.

28 Quoted in Geert Mak, *Amsterdam: A Brief Life of the City* (London: Vintage Books, 2001), 100.

29 *The Vocation and Mission of the Lay Faithful*, 26–7; *The Joy of the Gospel*, 114.

30 Angelus address, 16 March 2014.

31 Dublin: Columba, 2005.

32 For resources here, see Donal Harrington, *Eucharist: Enhancing the Prayer* (Dublin: Columba, 2007).

33 Francis, *The Joy of the Gospel*, 154.

34 See Donal Harrington, *Exploring Eucharist* (Dublin: Columba, 2007).

35 For resources, see Donal Harrington, *Weekday Prayers* (Dublin: Columba, 2013).

[36] Jean Vanier, *Man and Woman He Made Them* (London: Darton, Longman and Todd, 1985), 35, 39.

[37] *The Church in the Modern World*, 52; *Christian Education*, 3.

[38] Vatican II, *The Church*, 11; *The Laity*, 11.

[39] John Paul II, *The Christian Family in the Modern World* (1981), 13.

[40] *The Joy of the Gospel*, 76–109.

[41] *At the Dawn of a New Millennium*, 43.

[42] For resources, see Donal Harrington and Julie Kavanagh, *Prayer for Parish Groups* (Dublin: Columba, 1998); Donal Harrington, *Prayer Reflections for Group Meetings* (Dublin: Columba, 2004).

[43] *Code of Canon Law*, 536.2.

[44] See Donal Harrington, *The Welcoming Parish* (Dublin: Columba, 2005), 110–11.